Mediocracy

'*Mediocracy* will not be popular with educational and artistic bureaucrats, or with those who depend on them financially. Unlike official pronouncements on these matters, Tassano's entries are short, well-written, to the point and often amusing. They also provide well-chosen examples of the trends so many of us deplore.'

Professor Anthony O'Hear

'Tassano expertly skewers politically correct pomposity, and looks beyond the smooth, bland surface to the rough, pungent reality beneath our commonplace assumptions.'

Dr. Madsen Pirie, President, Adam Smith Institute

'As Tassano shows, the words we use really matter. Read this book and gain important insights into the way that the cultural elite's language works to disorient public debate.'

Professor Frank Furedi

'A remarkable indictment of our failure to protect proper standards. Tassano has mastered the evidence and details the sorry story stage by stage. Upsetting to read, and undoubtedly right.'

Alexander Deane, author of *The Great Abdication*

also by Fabian Tassano

The Power Of Life Or Death

'A terse, clear, incisive, intellectually first-class study of the growing power of doctors and of the lack of effective checks upon the too easily concealed but surely numerous abuses of that power.'

Professor Antony Flew

'His view goes straight to the medical jugular.'

Nature

'Tassano presents hair-raising case studies … his book is a timely polemic.'

Cristina Odone, *Literary Review*

'I would not recommend this book as comfortable bedtime reading … If you like an intellectual challenge this one is for you.'

British Medical Journal

Fabian Tassano

MEDIOCRACY

Inversions and deceptions
in an egalitarian culture

Oxford Forum

First published 2006 by Oxford Forum

© 2006 Fabian Wadel

Printed and bound in Wales by
Gomer Press, Llandysul, Ceredigion SA44 4JL

A catalogue record for this book is available from the British Library

Distributed by Book Systems Plus, Station Road, Linton, Cambs CB1 6NW, UK

ISBN-13: 978-0-953677-26-9
ISBN-10: 0-953677-26-5

Cover image: Henry Moore, *Reclining Figure* © Tate, London 2006,
reproduced by permission of the Henry Moore Foundation

Photograph of the author by Cherry-Ann Ballantyne LBIPP

www.celiagreen.com

MEDIOCRACY

Then will the earth have grown small, and upon it shall hop the Last Man who maketh all things small.

Nietzsche

A fable

Once upon a time there was a world which was culturally productive but rather inegalitarian, called Telluria. In Telluria, cultural progress depended on the existence of exceptional ability. Although innovations were often extended by the efforts of others, the original ideas for them came from a small number of highly gifted individuals.

The possession of exceptional ability in Telluria was predominantly a function of inherited characteristics, though favourable conditions could help. To be a cultural innovator required a high degree of innate talent and a high degree of innate ambition. If a Tellurian had those qualities, and was able to obtain opportunities to use them, they would become an innovator, otherwise they would not.

In any society, the opportunity to be culturally innovative requires freedom from having to earn a living in the conventional way. In Telluria this was possible because individuals were permitted to accumulate private surpluses, known as capital. Such surpluses arose because Telluria had markets for goods and services, and money as a medium for exchange. Private capital enabled a number of people to live as they pleased, without needing to satisfy the wishes of the community or its representatives.

Opportunities for a Tellurian innovator arose either when they acquired some capital, usually by gift or legacy from a relative; or when they were sponsored by a wealthy individual, usually in exchange for some rights in the resulting product. The fact that gift, legacy and sponsorship occurred in Telluria reflected a general recognition that abilities were innate, that culture depended on exceptional individuals who needed support, and that such support was not going to arise by any other means. It was accepted that there were differences in talent, and the existence of competition was regarded approvingly as a relatively benign expression of innate drives. The concept of the individual, as an entity distinct and independent from the community which contained him, was regarded as an important part of having a civilised society.

After a few centuries of markets and capital, Telluria had reached impressive levels of cultural output. Because of the heritability of talent and ambition, and the possibility of passing on the financial advantages acquired through aptitude, an entire social class developed in which exceptionality became relatively likely. This class became closely identified with the production of culture, and also with its consumption.

At first, the Tellurians were pleased with this outcome. It made them feel that theirs was a society to be admired and envied. The quality of life improved enormously, in terms of both necessities and leisure activities. Their culture stimulated and inspired the Tellurians, and encouraged them to have profound thoughts about life and the cosmos. It also increased their respect for the individual, which tended to make them behave somewhat better towards one another than they had previously done.

From the outset, however, there had been sceptics of culture who questioned the value of something which placed so much emphasis on the vision of individual innovators and which, the sceptics argued, threatened to undermine established values and hence the social cohesion of the community.

After a while, as culture and cultural innovators increasingly dominated the social and economic landscape, the sceptics' influence began to strengthen. More and more Tellurians began to feel uncomfortable with the degree of influence which innovators, and the class they mostly came from, had attained.

Some Tellurians began to question the existence of private surpluses. They began to regard it as inappropriate that some individuals were able to determine their lives without referring to the wishes of the community. They began to look back nostalgically to a time when that kind of autonomy would have been unthinkable. They began to argue that right and justice lay with the community as a whole, not with individuals, and that the community had lost its rightful claim to arrange everyone's lives as it saw fit.

This discomfort about culture, privacy and autonomy spread, and started to feed on the envy which many Tellurians felt for the advantages of the wealthy and for the special status of innovators. Tensions also developed among the new culture-oriented social class as it expanded. Some of its members started to worry that a finite amount of reward for innovation was being divided among an increasing number of potential innovators. They sensed that their status needed to be protected, and that this could be achieved by maligning rival innovators, or even by attacking their own class.

In response to these tensions, Telluria began to develop an ideology which proclaimed the virtues and rights of the community, and which denigrated the significance of the individual. As this ideology was elaborated, it increasingly queried the supposed merits of the prevailing economic system. It questioned whether markets satisfied genuine wants or simply manipulated people's foolishness, and whether the distribution of surpluses reflected anything that could be ethically or even economically defended.

It was pointed out that economic inequalities between people, which resulted from the interaction between individual differences in ability and the workings of the markets, were not ones which had been explicitly sanctioned by the community. Inequality, both economic and cultural, began to be criticised. Any attitude which appeared to justify the existence of either type of inequality was attacked as 'elitist'.

The cultural benefits of the existing system were also disputed. It was debated whether culture was worth having if it appealed differentially to different classes. It was questioned whether 'quality' meant anything with regard to culture, or whether any product with recognisably cultural features should count as good culture. It was particularly questioned whether cultural output depended on exceptional individuals, as had been thought – and indeed whether the concept of 'exceptional individual' was meaningful – or whether these were simply myths created to justify a dubious social system.

A new philosophy started to become dominant, according to which the opinion of the community – meaning the opinion of an elite who (it was supposed) represented community interests – was the appropriate criterion of what should happen in every area of life. The opinion of the elite was also increasingly taken to be the appropriate criterion for deciding what was true or real.

❁   ❁   ❁

In spite of their enthusiasm for egalitarianism, and their rejection of exceptionality, the Tellurians wanted their world to continue having activities they could identify as culture and cultural progress. This was partly so they would not feel they had lost anything, and partly so that their society could not be criticised by outsiders.

They therefore developed a substitute culture, financed from the public purse, which they argued was just as good as the original. In fact, they claimed, it was in many ways better. It was less elitist, because it tended to be that either the majority of people enjoyed it or, more typically, that no one did. It was more sophisticated, because it involved more technology and was often expensive. And it could be regarded as more progressive, because it tended to undermine the old beliefs about culture, markets and the significance of the individual.

This replacement of old culture with new required the redefinition of many old concepts, in line with the new, revolutionary philosophy. For example, since 'reality' was now understood to mean 'the world view of the elite', the meanings of teaching and learning had to be moved away from 'acquisition of facts' and towards 'acquisition of socially approved viewpoints'. Art, music and theatre were no longer about subjective aesthetics or private enjoyment but about the expression of political positions, and existed primarily in order to challenge the old-fashioned social order. To analyse or criticise came to mean, 'to question references to pre-revolutionary concepts'.

As the idea of being able to assess culture objectively was progressively abandoned, the criterion for what constituted 'good' economics (physics, philosophy, literary criticism etc.) became that of whether the techniques used were those currently approved by the community of socially accredited economists (physicists, philosophers, literary critics etc.). Technique therefore became very important as a marker of quality, and as a result became so complex that even accredited practitioners had difficulty comprehending the output of their own disciplines.

However, after a few decades of this pseudoculture, which was predominantly boring and/or repellent, Tellurians became disillusioned with the whole idea of culture, and henceforth restricted themselves to a diet of soap operas, game shows and pop music.

mediocracy

n. 1 the rule of the mediocre.

    2 the triumph of style over substance.

The following is a guide to cultural terminology in a mediocracy. For each term, the entry gives examples of incorrect and correct usage, one or more illustrative quotations, and commentary about the term and associated phenomena.

Where a word is printed like *this*, it is being used in its mediocratic sense, which is likely to differ significantly from the original meaning. The reader should refer to the relevant entry for the appropriate definition.

Ability

 Innate quality enabling a person to excel in a number of areas.

 Tendency to perform well at a specific task as a result of training.

No one has ever created outstanding accomplishments without undergoing a lengthy period of careful preparation. Ordinary people can gain the same skills that have been cited as proof that an individual was innately gifted.

Professor Michael Howe

I n a mediocracy, we are required to think of ourselves as products of society. The concept of innate ability is considered threatening, as it implies an area that society may not be able to control. A simple way of minimising the significance of intrinsic differences between individuals is to stress those aspects of the person common to everyone, e.g. physiology, ageing, sex.

Mediocratic **research** is devoted to the thesis that apparent ability is the result of a favourable environment. In other words, that anyone can be a political leader, intellectual or artist, if only provided with suitable conditions.

Abuse

 Hostility towards bourgeois individuals.

 Behaviour within the family that conflicts with contemporary concepts of fairness.

> Nobel Prize winner Elfriede Jelinek's depiction of abuse derives from her understanding of capitalism. Her characters are incapable of liberation because they have internalised a consumer ideology that treats people as objects to be accumulated or discarded.
>
> *The Literary Encyclopedia*

Mediocracy poses as the champion of empathy and tolerance. Its cultural output, on the other hand, more often expresses *assertiveness* (i.e. aggression). Ostensibly the assertiveness is aimed at the enemies of egalitarianism – men, capitalists, conservatives, the bourgeoisie. Ultimately, however, everyone is considered a fair target.

Behind the rhetoric against abuse, an increase in interpersonal aggression is actually regarded as desirable. It helps to destabilise the private sphere and can be used to justify intervention. However, condemning aggression in specific circumstances is a useful way of attacking things that are not sufficiently communal, particularly family relationships.

Academia

 Environment which provides intellectuals with administrative and domestic support.

 State institution for generating ideologically appropriate research.

> American philosophy is a vast and industrious enterprise. There are 10,000 professional academic philosophers. About 4,000 new philosophical books and articles are published every year.
>
> *Philosophy for Beginners*

Old-fashioned academia provided freedom for what mediocracy considers the wrong sort of people, i.e. those with their own minds. The updated version contains a profusion of highly trained mediocrities, and exists to generate ***research*** that is sufficiently vacuous to be unthreatening. As with other areas of culture, an ersatz version more effectively displaces the genuine form than does simple suppression.

If ten thousand professional philosophers wrote five academic papers a year for a hundred years, might one of the papers contain a profound observation? Perhaps, but if so it would be an unintended result from the point of view of mediocracy.

Academic

 Intellectual provided with resources to use his abilities in the way he sees fit.

 Trained person employed to publish papers and maintain high standards of *awareness*.

> Academics should have less freedom of expression than writers and artists because they are supposed to be creating a better world.
>
> Professor Barbara Johnson, Harvard

The ideal academic in a mediocracy is a highly trained hack. Someone with some intelligence but negligible interest in reality. Someone who can crank out verbiage with a sheen of respectability, but who does not want to make intellectual progress.

The safest kind of academic output is that which says nothing at all, but in a way that demonstrates facility with the techniques *du jour*. That is usually sufficient to permit ascension of the career ladder. More points can, however, be scored with output that conveys the correct sentiments or that generates desirable conclusions.

The mediocratic attitude to academics who do not generate ideologically acceptable material at a sufficient rate is that they should not be promoted, or should be relegated to the fringes of the system. Those who go so far as to contradict the ideology will be sacked.

Academic theory

 Models for explaining the world.

 The abstract ruminations of academics, intended to demonstrate technical expertise.

> Literary theory is unsettling. It brings assumptions into question, in what is often a forbidding and arcane style. Of course theory is difficult, but simply assuming that it is all empty rhetoric keeps you from confronting the real questions that it raises.
>
> *Critical Terms for Literary Study*

The purpose of mediocratic theory – whether in physics, economics, or literary studies – is to reinforce the mediocratic ethos. Theoretical output must comply with the following principles to ensure that this goal is met.

- Complex terminology must be employed.
- Mathematical symbolism should be used if possible.
- Meaning must be either obscure or, ideally, absent.
- An *egalitarian* and/or *physicalist* perspective should be conveyed, preferably by implication rather than explicitly.
- Bourgeois values should be attacked, or at least not supported.
- One should aim for a tone of grim seriousness, although
- humour may be used to deflate, provided the targets of deflation are bourgeois concepts, e.g. 'freedom', 'objectivity'.

Accessibility

 'Cultural output should be comprehensible and appealing.'

 'Cultural output can only be understood by the trained, but this category should include all social groups in the correct proportions.'

> Under New Labour, museums and galleries are required to classify their visitors by class and ethnicity and then seek to mirror in their attendance the proportion of each of the designated groups within society as a whole.
>
> *Guardian*

Accessibility of culture is an oxymoron in a mediocracy. Mediocratic high culture is not accessible, even to relatively intelligent people, nor is it intended to be.

Mediocracy proclaims its rejection of elitism. What it actually rejects is not elitism but a particular kind of culture – the kind which might make people feel good, or illuminated, in undesirable ways. Demanding accessibility is a useful way of degrading or eliminating such culture.

To the extent it is retained, the old bourgeois culture must be **cartoonised** in order to fit with egalitarian ideology. By contrast, there is little attempt to make the new mediocratic culture more digestible, as it can safely be assumed that such culture is already conveying the correct messages.

Achievement

 High level of success.

 Sense of well-being which the state should arrange for everyone to experience.

> We need a curriculum which redefines achievement away from its current narrow academic connotations. One which encourages achievement for *all* and which promotes creativity, collaboration and a sense of adventure.
>
> National Union of Teachers

Real achievement is regarded as undesirable in a mediocracy, as it has the potential of making people feel *special,* i.e. too different from others. In its place, there are to be undemanding targets which everyone can meet, provided they first acquire approved training.

To complain that this represents excessive individualism or mollycoddling is to misunderstand the mediocratic agenda. The objective is not to make anyone feel better about themselves. It is to emphasise that there is only one permissible aspiration: to consider oneself no worse, but no better, than anyone else.

Aesthetic

 Referring to objective properties of beauty, quality, craftsmanship, etc.

 Applied to a product which conforms to professional standards of acceptability.

> Taste functions as a sort of social orientation, implying a practical anticipation of what the social meaning of the chosen thing will probably be.
>
> Pierre Bourdieu

The old idea of aesthetics as reflecting innate psychological preferences is to be rejected, as it places too much faith in the judgement of individuals. Instead, state-approved experts must tell people what they ought to consider artistic.

What passes the mediocratic criterion for art is that which has the appropriate ideological effect. To be uplifted by art is too pro-individualistic. It is better that art should make the viewer feel ill, as this will reduce the risk of his being inspired, or of otherwise becoming self-assertive. Good mediocratic art should make the audience accept their subordination to the physical, and to society.

Aid

 Helping other countries in temporary distress.

 Action which increases global equality.

> Providing aid is an obligation and a matter of justice, not an act of charity. At the UN General Assembly in 2000, the world's governments recognised their collective responsibility to uphold equality at the global level.
>
> Oxfam

Mediocratic 'aid' provides a useful rationale for removing assets from the bourgeoisie, with the potential for broader use than the more local concept of *welfare*.

For a society which loves the trite and hates complexity, the concept of helping people with lives radically different from one's own is attractive. While it may be hard to avoid noticing that the effects of welfare in one's own country are mixed, it is easy for someone to judge about some far off community, 'these conditions are unacceptable (to me)', and to decide that other people should be forced to pay for change.

Evidence that *aid* does not work is considered irrelevant. The point is not to achieve anything but to make an ideological statement. I.e. that people with more autonomy than the global minimum ought to surrender some of it, regardless of whether or not doing so increases the autonomy of others.

Analysis

 Applying thought to something and checking whether it makes sense.

 Demonstrating that capitalism is oppressive, using methods independent of bourgeois logic.

> The move from a structuralist account in which capital is understood to structure social relations in relatively homologous ways to a view of hegemony in which power relations are subject to repetition, convergence, and rearticulation brought the question of temporality into the thinking of structure, and marked a shift from a form of Althusserian theory that takes structural totalities as theoretical objects to one in which the insights into the contingent possibility of structure inaugurate a renewed conception of hegemony as bound up with the contingent sites and strategies of the rearticulation of power. [sic]
>
> Professor Judith Butler, Berkeley

Old-fashioned analysis was unhelpful, as it allowed the individual to question socially agreed beliefs. In a mediocracy, criticism is desirable only in carefully selected areas.

The mediocratic version of analysis is designed to be usable only for criticising capitalism. It is incomprehensible, in order to prevent anyone from analysing *it*.

Anger

 Reaction to finding modern society boring, pointless and without scope for drive.

 Reaction to having insufficient opportunities provided for one by the state.

Q. What should we think about Muslim terrorists?

A. What people are angry about is political inequity, economic inequity, and dictators who keep all the money for the upper classes and leave their nations impoverished.

Professor Anisa Mehdi

Mediocracy teaches that a high level of autonomy implies exploitation of others. This ideology is used to legitimise hostility towards those with autonomy, and is then extended to legitimise hostility in *any* context, provided there is an implied demand for more, rather than less, activity on the part of the collective.

Anger is encouraged where its targets are individuals, especially bourgeois individuals: individual businessmen, landowners, politicians, parents. Anger is also acceptable if targeted at groups whose views are at variance with some aspect of mediocratic ideology: critics of interventionism, cultural conservatives, creationists, environmental sceptics, etc.

However, hostility towards socially acceptable groups or professions is taboo. Anger against the cultural establishment, against oppressive religions or cultures, against the medical profession, against academia – such anger is out of touch, prejudiced, or a sign of social inadequacy.

Appearance

☒ **The superficial aspect of things.**

☑ **The aspect of things that is easiest to verify socially, and which therefore matters most.**

> Baudrillard's recurrent theme is the disappearance of the real, and the reign of appearance. He suggests that truth and reality are illusions, and that people should respect appearance, and give up the quest for truth and reality.
>
> *Stanford Encyclopedia of Philosophy*

In mediocracy what matters is what the majority thinks, or what it can be manipulated into thinking. Social consensus is the only criterion of reality. Since society sees what is presented rather than what is behind the image, appearance becomes more important than substance. Naming and labelling are social activities; their significance therefore outweighs the question of content. Similarly, socially conferred status outweighs innate ability.

We must not be reminded that there might be a type of reality other than the superficial one. There must therefore be appropriate conceptual **blurring** between appearance and reality. Who knows what anything really means, say mediocratic philosophers, while being careful to retain their belief in the importance of **aid**, gender equality, etc.

Art

 Visual product that employs principles of aesthetics to stimulate mental activity.

 Visual product that subverts or politicises, and is deemed 'art' by an approved institution.

> Progressive art can assist people to learn about the intensely social character of their interior lives.
>
> Professor Angela Davis, University of California

> There is in fact no such thing as art for art's sake, art that stands above classes, art that is detached from or independent of politics.
>
> Chairman Mao, Little Red Book

The mediocratic criterion of art, as of all high culture, is based on **technicality** rather than aesthetics, i.e. on consistency with currently fashionable trends. It does not matter if art is horrible or disgusting, as long as it demonstrates the methods and references approved by the professional art community.

One method particularly likely to gain approval is 'subversion'. But only subversion of things which are safe to subvert, e.g. capitalism or bourgeois culture. Never subversion of the central tenets of mediocracy, such as **equality**.

The purpose of art in a mediocracy is not to enlighten or illuminate. It is to make people feel they are subordinated to material and social forces. Most mediocratic art fulfils this function well, and can therefore be described as 'good' art, on mediocratic terms.

Artist

 Individual who produces artistic work.

 Individual sanctioned by the collective to manufacture visual products.

> I don't think art is necessarily about skill. It might be about semantics or about putting two things together.
>
> Cornelia Parker, artist

> Artists cannot ignore what is going on around them. An artist must be reminded of his duty, perhaps rather firmly. He is working for his people.
>
> Joseph Goebbels

The old-fashioned idea of artists – exceptional individuals free to pursue their creative drives without reference to society – is considered dubious in a mediocracy, as it conflicts with concepts such as *awareness* and *responsibility*. However, two ersatz versions will be permitted.

First, there will be support of approved *serious* artists, who need not have much originality but must convey the right ideological messages.

Second, the market is permitted to support the output of *popular* artists. Market-driven art is tolerated because of mediocracy's redistributive policies, which ensure that markets reflect the tastes of the mass rather than that of the bourgeoisie.

Assertiveness

 Attitude involving protection of one's interests.

 Aggression legitimised by reference to egalitarian or anti-bourgeois standards.

Anyone here liked *The Remains of the Day*? Get the f*** outta here!

Quentin Tarantino at screening of *Pulp Fiction*

In Helen Zahavi's novel *Dirty Weekend*, a young woman is pestered by dirty phone calls. Eventually, she enters the culprit's flat through a window and batters his head with a hammer. The book has been praised by Andrea Dworkin as "good" and "true".

Wikipedia

Mediocracy likes to promote resentful belligerence towards other individuals as a form of self-assertion. Manners and self-restraint are examples of bourgeois fetishism and hence to be rejected.

Aside from actual or threatened violence, the belligerence can take more sophisticated forms such as rudeness, or attempts to degrade or belittle. More subtly still, it can be expressed in the form of a coercive world view: for example, demanding that people subscribe to *physicalism*.

Ultimately, 'assertiveness' is unavoidable for someone living in a mediocracy, as it becomes the only practical way of dealing with everyone else's assertiveness.

Authentic

 Real, genuine, not pretentious or phoney.

✓ **Referring to violence, sex or social issues.**

> The Tate show 'In-A-Gadda-Da-Vida' contains a giant block of Spam, a bucket representing the Virgin Mary's vagina, a masturbating bomb, the pubic hair of Adam and Eve, a bloke on a toilet, and the inside of a lorry-driver's cab plastered with pornographic cuttings from the tabloids.
>
> *Sunday Times*

The real in a mediocracy becomes synonymous with *the wretched* and *the sordid*. Proletarian reality is the only authentic reality, notwithstanding the fact that the concept of 'proletarian' invoked is largely mythical.

This goal of pseudo-proletarianisation is one key to understanding the content of mediocratic culture. More sex, more horror, more degradation: a blow against the hated bourgeois intellectual.

Being authentic comes to mean being willing to violate bourgeois sensitivities, and to rub the audience's nose in what it is fashionable to consider as real.

Author

 Creator of cultural work.

 Spurious term which fails to recognise that the origin of a cultural product is society.

The text is a tissue of quotations drawn from the innumerable centres of culture.

Roland Barthes, 'The death of the author'

A number of arguments militate against a text being written by an intentional individual. The concept of the stable ego has been challenged – it has been suggested that 'we' are in fact processes of symbolisation. The idea of 'the individual' has been seen as an ideological conception, a product of capitalist revolution in the seventeenth century.

Professor John Lye, Brock University

Mediocracy requires the pretensions of the bourgeois intellectual to be crushed. It must be realised that such individuals have no claim to special conditions. They are not to be regarded even as the originators of the works that have their names on them.

When analysing literature, what is to count is not the intentions of the author, but how the text can be linked to political preoccupations.

Autism

 Serious cognitive disorder.

 Tendency to avoid social interaction.

> The eccentric behaviour of Einstein and Newton could have been caused by autism, claims leading specialist Professor Simon Baron-Cohen of Cambridge University. Both had problems communicating, had obsessive interests and experienced difficulties in social relationships.
>
> *Daily Telegraph*

In mediocracy, the ability to interact socially becomes the standard for assessing the individual, rather than intellectual or other skills.

Those who are unable, or unwilling, to engage in social interaction of a kind recognised as normal are to be treated as suspect. A psychopathological term of sufficient vagueness can be a useful label for implying incompatibility with mediocratic values.

Autonomy

 The ability to make decisions about one's life free from interference by others.

 A person's feeling (achieved with the help of experts) that he is exercising choice.

We can help others attain an autonomous life by educating them, or by providing them with options from which to choose their preferred lifestyle. The government may have to create the conditions under which citizens can act autonomously.

Professor Simon Lee

In the same institutions in which corporate culture is dominant, the highest levels of true autonomy occur. For example, a Tupperware dealer says, "the company gives me great freedom to develop my own approach. If you choose the colours – I prefer lavender and lace – that's okay."

Peters and Waterman, *In Search of Excellence*

Rather than condemning individualistic concepts such as autonomy, mediocracy prefers to redefine them.

Mediocratic autonomy is not about a person doing what he wants, but about the community helping him to make socially acceptable choices, and ensuring that he experiences an appropriate *sense* of self-determination.

Awareness

☒	**State of being well informed.**
☑	**State of being attuned to egalitarian principles and the oppressiveness of capitalism.**

> I'm helping Amnesty International build a new Human Rights Action Centre, including a 'School of Activism' where people of all ages can learn how to make a real, tangible difference for the better in the world.
>
> Anita Roddick DBE

Mediocracy has a particular idea about which aspects of reality one needs to be aware of. Ideologically neutral facts about the world are relatively unimportant. In any case, notions such as 'neutral' or 'objective' are regarded as dubious.

The reality considered relevant is data conducive to the promotion of egalitarianism. One is, for instance, allowed to reflect on the bad conditions of the working class under industrialisation and before social reform, but not the bad conditions prior to capitalism or under alternative economic systems. One may debate the absence of civil liberties under colonialism, but not their absence under pre-colonial or post-colonial regimes.

To be considered 'aware' requires not only knowledge of the right kinds of data, but commitment to *progress* – i.e. reforming society by means of ideology or, if necessary, *crisis*.

'Black'

 Equally able to embrace bourgeois culture.

 Supportive of egalitarian values.

The 2005 election ushers in the first 'black' Tory MP, for a party which repudiates equality and diversity policies. The victor deserves to be despised by egalitarians and people who believe in human rights.

Yasmin Alibhai-Brown, Independent

African-American men seemed to understand it right away: white skin notwithstanding, Bill Clinton was our first black President.

Professor Toni Morrison, Princeton

In a mediocracy, a black *individual* is viewed no more sympathetically than any other individual. Mediocratic ethics concerns itself exclusively with groups. But the concept of 'black' can be a useful symbol for a certain kind of politics.

Mediocracy encourages guilt towards other racial groups, by stressing supposed wrongs committed in the past, and by making everyone anxious about being racist. Having sensitised its audience, it likes to indoctrinate it with a particular version of 'black culture'. Ethnic culture which advances *egalitarian* values is cheered and promoted, but blacks who identify with bourgeois values are shunned.

Blurring

 Undesirable confusion between fact and fiction.

 Feature of cultural output in which reality and fantasy are mixed together in exciting ways.

> Philip Pullman's *His Dark Materials* offers a subtle way to introduce youngsters to some of the most exciting ideas in physics. It is a gift to any teacher trying to fire the imagination of budding physicists.
>
> Dr. John Gribbin

The idea that there is an objective reality independent of social agreement, which individuals can assess for themselves, is rejected in a mediocracy. The blurring of the boundary between reality and fantasy is encouraged, as a way of undermining the old bourgeois concept of objectivity. Confusing people about what is truth and what is fiction is helpful in promoting the social model of reality.

However, blurring must not be applied to inappropriate areas. Playing with the question of 'what is real?' must not be allowed to undermine the core beliefs of mediocracy, e.g. *egalitarianism*.

Body

 The physical aspect of a person, as distinct from the mental.

 Another word for 'person'.

> In a disused abattoir, two men dive into a pool of broken glass and start backstroking. As they clamber out, blood drips from their backs. One of the men breaks paving slabs on the other's head. The older man sticks a pin through his own throat. Then he attaches hooks to the flesh of his back.
>
> Review of performance art

In a mediocracy, people are defined in terms of their bodies. Cultural output revolves around themes that emphasise our physicality: sex, physiology, death, medicine.

The body is highlighted in contrast to the mind because this helps to promote the belief that we are all *equal*, i.e. equally degraded and equally amenable to social manipulation.

Boggling

 Pointless rumination about the difficulty of defining things.

 A sign of social awareness.

> We are in a crisis of meaning. What do our
> institutions mean? What does it mean to be educated?
> What does it mean in today's world to be human?
> I want a society that fills us up again and makes us feel
> part of something bigger than ourselves.
>
> Hillary Clinton

Bourgeois culture can be undermined by encouraging a certain type of pseudo-philosophical doubt. This kind of scepticism needs to applied selectively, however. It would not do to query attempts to solve global poverty, for example.

In some cases, boggling generates unanswerable questions, and hence engenders intellectual capitulation. This is helpful to mediocracy, as it can be used to encourage unthinking acceptance of the prevailing ideology.

In other cases, the purpose of boggling is to block real questioning, by signalling that an issue has become taboo. *What are universities for?* it is asked, for example. But there is no intention of considering as a possible answer: *for giving scope to the most intelligent*, as this answer conflicts with mediocratic ideology. Such boggling helps to confuse potential critics, if they are ingenuous enough to believe it constitutes genuine deliberation or openness to debate.

Brutality

 Harshness of a type which a civilised society repudiates, and avoids visually representing.

 Aspect of reality which should be shown in full detail in order to achieve authenticity.

A character on a TV show is shown being tied up and skinned alive, his remains incinerated. In a spy drama, a woman has her teeth pulled out as a form of torture. In another TV drama, a captive, who can breathe only through straws in her nose, is chained, beaten, and finally suffocated.

Christian Science Monitor

Mediocratic culture likes to confront its audience with horror and degradation, under cover of *realism*. Brutal violence is gleefully portrayed in drama that wants to lay claim to authenticity. Reactions of disgust are rejected as bourgeois hypersensitivity.

The psychological purpose is to make people feel helpless and at the mercy of their physiology. If sadism and other underclass phenomena are incidentally legitimised, so much the better.

Intentionally shocking representations may be rationalised by reference to the author's supposed disapproval of what is being portrayed. However, the emotional effect on the audience of seeing, say, a person's ear sliced off – if not simply repulsion – is typically amusement, tolerance, or desensitisation.

Business

 Essential part of society.

Morally dubious activity, allowed on sufferance.

> By means of greater regulation, corporations are turned into our slaves. Instead of draining wealth from the poor, they are forced to return it. Many, perhaps most, will go under in the attempt, and we should delight to see them drown.
>
> George Monbiot

Mediocracy stigmatises and penalises commercial activity, but its penalty system is designed to favour some kinds of commerce over others.

A person running their own business is automatically an object of suspicion. A large corporation also qualifies for hostility, but in that case there are potential extenuating factors. Mediocracy knows it cannot do without business – who else is going to produce the leisure products for the mass to consume? At least, it insists, we must have business with communitarian values. In other words, business should be large, and it should encourage its staff to embrace a collectivist culture. Everyone must absorb the values of their employer.

We are permitted to draw attention to the authoritarianism practised by large corporations, but only if we blame 'capitalism' for those practices, rather than mediocratic ideology.

Capitalism

 Free markets with minimal state intervention.

✓ **System in which cultural output is dominated by the spending power of the mass.**

> Wealth is unjust where it arises not from hard work and risk-taking enterprise, but from brute luck factors. Inheritance is a form of brute-luck inequality, enabling citizens to share in the social product while violating reciprocity.
>
> Professor Anthony Giddens

What mediocracy dislikes about old-style capitalism is that exceptional individuals were sometimes able to act independently of the social will, using money accumulated by their families or supporters. Provided this possibility is curtailed by taxing capital, markets for goods can be tolerated. Indeed, they can be regarded as a force for good (i.e. working in favour of mediocracy), once policies have shifted spending power sufficiently towards the mass.

By referring to this reconstructed system by the old name, dissatisfaction can be directed at the original concept. Thus 'capitalism' is cited to be the source of most problems, from dumbing down, to environmental damage, to the health problems of employees. The mediocratic elite are happy to play along with this confusion. Any cultural producer who wants to be taken seriously is required to take a dim view of 'capitalism', without however letting his audience think too much about what the word actually means.

Caring

 Doing something to help an individual in need.

☑ **Demanding that other people contribute to causes considered deserving by the majority.**

> Celebrity agents offer clients a charity matching service to ensure the 'best fit' for their target demographic. It is a symbiotic relationship: charities need profile and celebrities need meaning.
>
> *New Statesman*

There is much talk of *caring* in a mediocracy. The sort of caring meant, however, is rather specific. It has little to do with helping acquaintances in need, or giving money to a single homeless person. These private acts are not sufficiently communal. If people need help, it should be provided only by those who know best.

Instead of private charity, individuals are encouraged to support *institutionalised* aid. The form of the aid is to be decided by trained experts, not by the victims themselves.

This collective form of 'help' becomes the new ethical norm. Guilt should not be felt for failing to help someone who asks for assistance, but for failing to vote for a party that supports higher taxes to finance more *welfare* and *aid*.

Cartoonisation

 Reducing things to crude stereotypes for the benefit of a dumbed down audience.

 Making things more digestible and fun.

> There was a documentary last night which showed footage of happy slapping. Because each new incident has to be better than the last, they are now pulling people off bicycles and setting fire to tramps, etc. One of the kids said it was funny because it was like what he saw on the television.
>
> Weblog

In mediocratic drama, individuals are two-dimensional and fall into a few crude categories (he-man, psychopath, nerd, vamp, virgin, etc.). Complex interests are boiled down to primitive urges (sex, aggression, money). Motives and narratives are reduced to the formulaic. The lurid, the grotesque and the funny is emphasised. Detailed characterisation is scrupulously avoided.

Outside fiction, cartoonisation is equally prevalent. Historical figures are reinterpreted in simplistic terms. We want to know whether they were disturbed, perverted or obnoxious, but are not particularly interested in the details of what they achieved.

Cartoonisation comes to affect the way people view contemporary events. Violence, horror and suffering are perceived as unaffecting or even humorous, unless they come clearly labelled 'socially sanctioned as requiring sympathy', e.g. disasters in the developing world.

Celebrity

 Person regarded as significant because of their achievements or talent.

 Person with sufficient media exposure for the mass to be interested in their personal life.

Stuck in a dead end job with no prospects?
Unemployed or drifting through school unfulfilled?
SpringBoard UK is a new service for people like you
wanting to become famous. No longer is this fantastic
career path a closed shop. Now anyone can be a star!

SpringBoard UK

I n a mediocracy we are sceptical of innate exceptionality. However, we retain our taste for celebrity, which we come to see as manufactured by ourselves. Although we may retain some interest in the idea of superior quality, it becomes important to prove that prominence is essentially controlled by us. We prove this by assigning it with increasing arbitrariness.

Not only *can* every ordinary person become famous, but this model of fame displaces the original one. Extraordinariness becomes irrelevant to the issue.

Challenge

 To question the values of the cultural establishment.

 To reject bourgeois traditions, essential part of any cultural activity.

A good starting place for intellectual subversion is to get pupils to ask: "Why are you teaching this to me today?" We have found that, when pupils and teachers together explore learning, some of the most deeply ingrained beliefs are opened to question.

John MacBeath, Cambridge Professor of Education

Mediocracy has ersatz versions of everything related to intellectual independence: questioning, analysis, scepticism, radicalism, and so on. No real questioning or analysis is involved, since that would be too dangerous.

There are two reasons for a culture of pseudo-analysis. First, having a replacement version is safer than trying to eliminate openly. The latter would make it too obvious that something was being suppressed. By suitable redefinition, it becomes impossible to complain that an activity (e.g. *real* challenge) is in fact absent.

Second, the energies of those who might in other circumstances be doing the real questioning, challenging etc. need to be safely absorbed by being directed towards attacking the enemies of mediocracy.

Child

 Young person requiring management by parents.

 Young person requiring management by state agents, including behavioural medication.

The very notion of a child is historically and culturally conditioned.

Professor Gareth Matthews

Soviet propaganda encouraged collective education of even the youngest children, and family ties were often represented as a bourgeois survival.

Kolakowski, *Main Currents of Marxism*

The concept of childhood is sometimes said to be a creation of the Victorians. This is usually intended to demonstrate its artificiality. More plausibly, it reflects the relative enthusiasm of that time for a private realm into which social claims are not permitted to intrude. This private aspect of childhood also explains the mediocratic attitude to the concept, which is that it should be presumed to be illusory – except when it can be used as a justification for intervention.

Mediocracy requires that there be no special loyalties between parents and children. If children have needs, it is the state which will assume responsibility, even if it has to compel the services of biological parents in order to fulfil those responsibilities.

Childhood

 Stage when a person should be exposed to relatively little sex and violence.

 Stage when a person should be socialised by state educators and receive sexual training.

> These days children's books are a hell of a lot more explicit about sex, and expressive of hardcore social issues. According to Professor Nicholas Tucker, children's books have to be grim to explain issues that parents shirk from discussing.
>
> *Spectator*

Mediocracy does not like the idea that children should be exempt from public scrutiny. One must think of them as little adults, in the sense that they should be as subjected to social evaluation as everyone else.

Children, like adults, must be exposed to *realism* and other aspects of the prevailing ideology. Otherwise there is a risk they could escape indoctrination with the appropriate mediocratic values, at the most crucial stage of life.

Child-centred

 Term for a process which is adapted to the wishes of the individual child.

 Term for a process which elicits, by careful questioning, the correct answer from a child.

If you 'police' a pupil's prejudiced remarks too heavily this may result in them resentfully confirming their prejudice. Try using an open question, e.g. 'what messages do we receive from the media about girls?' You could get pupils to brainstorm this, and then run a discussion on the negativity of these messages.

National Children's Bureau

The extreme doctrines handed down to schools in Britain and America were an expression of a cultural shift that was the apotheosis of individualism.

Melanie Phillips

Mediocracy advertises itself as supportive of autonomy and as opposed to indoctrination. This pretence is accepted even by its opponents, with the result that any criticism of mediocracy can only be expressed as opposition to 'individualism'.

In fact, mediocracy's claims of being patient-centred, child-centred and so on are spurious. Self-determination is tolerated only if it is aimed in approved directions.

The confusion of mediocratic liberalism with genuine liberty is not accidental. Provoking attacks on individualism by generating a negative version of it is an astute strategy.

Christianity

 Belief in the divinity of Jesus.

 Belief in the importance of social justice.

> The scandal of our current global economy is that it leaves children dying, it leaves over a billion in extreme need. The rich protect their markets while talking about the virtues of free trade.
>
> Dr. Rowan Williams, Archbishop of Canterbury

> In case we cannot understand 'O Lord, open thou our lips,' the *Guide to Common Worship* suggests we use, 'We say hello!' And confession is retitled, 'doing the dirt on ourselves.'
>
> Revd. Dr. Peter Mullen

Christianity, with its belief in individual responsibility and individual salvation, is a potential source of opposition to mediocratic ideology.

Indeed, *any* system which has an intellectual philosophy of some kind, and behaves as if it thinks its views are important, is a threat to an ethos which depends on the idea that nothing matters except social consensus.

Christianity therefore needs to be neutralised in some way. This is best achieved by modification and redefinition rather than elimination. What kind of Christianity can a mediocratic society tolerate? One which focuses exclusively on *equality* and *fairness*.

Clever

 Possessing critical faculties, including the ability to see through nonsense.

 Able to employ and manipulate the concepts and terminology of an academic discipline.

> Judith Butler* is probably one of the ten smartest people on the planet.
>
> Professor Warren Hedges

Thinking is not considered desirable in a mediocracy – particularly thinking by intellectuals, since it generates a risk that the deceptions of mediocracy will be unmasked, or that alternative perspectives will be conceived.

Mediocracy cannot permit real intellectuals to be recognised as such, in case their views are taken seriously by others. It therefore needs to create replacement versions of 'intelligence' and 'intellectual'. In place of the ability to penetrate reality, we substitute a talent for acquiring conventions, and the ability to manipulate currently fashionable terminology.

---

* See *Analysis*.

Consciousness

 Central continuous element of an individual.

 Illusory phenomenon that appears to emerge as a result of social interaction.

> Admitting that consciousness is an illusion changes the problem completely. Instead of asking how neural impulses turn into experiences, we must ask how the grand illusion gets constructed. Unlike solving the former problem, this task may at least be possible.
>
> Dr. Susan Blackmore

A key element of the mediocratic worldview is the rejection of the individual as a meaningful entity. Mind, consciousness, the unity of the self: these are to be called into question, and attacked as devices for reinforcing bourgeois ideology.

The rejection of consciousness is supported by the pseudo-analyses of mediocratic philosophy. If consciousness appears difficult to accommodate within existing science, this is taken as evidence that it does not exist, rather than raising the possibility that the prevailing scientific model is too limited.

Conservatism

 Philosophy which believes in free markets and minimal state intervention.

 Movement which seeks to outdo socialism on issues such as regulation and censorship.

We believe people must have every opportunity to fulfil their potential. We believe in equality of opportunity. Injustice makes us angry.

Michael Howard

School-leavers could be forced to do four months community work under a Conservative government, David Cameron has said. "One of the biggest issues in the UK is lack of social cohesion."

BBC News

The true test of an ideology's hegemony is the degree to which its enemies feel they can criticise it only on *its* terms, or oppose it only by relinquishing their original principles. In this way, mediocracy's would-be opponents become implicit defenders of the status quo.

There are two preferred positions for the enemies of mediocracy. They can reinforce the mediocratic position by demonstrating a complete lack of self-belief. "Don't support us", they imply, "we are not worthy". Alternatively, they can play by the prevailing ideological rules, and compete by offering a more aggressive brand of mediocracy, with emphasis on authoritarianism and/or military activity. Either way, the dominance of mediocracy is reinforced.

Conservative

 Person who supports conservatism.

 Person who is insufficiently egalitarian and ineligible for positions in cultural institutions.

"I don't agree with your personal preferences," my first-year student confidently responded to my suggestions. I saw my years of teaching experience dissolve before my eyes.

I worry people may think I am a cultural conservative, but I consider myself a progressive in social, political, and pedagogical matters.

Susan Weisser, American Professor of English

Mediocracy cannot permit genuine dissent. Apart from the fact that its ideology must not be questioned, there is the risk that its high culture will be exposed as valueless.

The solution is to create an ethic according to which any deviation from the consensus is treated as opposition to *egalitarianism*, to *progress*, and to *fairness*. The description 'conservative' does not necessarily mean much beyond a failure to subscribe to the prevailing cultural shibboleths. However, to be labelled as such becomes anathema in most cultural professions.

Under mediocracy we may hear mutterings about a hiring bias in cultural institutions, but these are misconceived. Discrimination requires an alternative to be discriminated against. In a mediocracy there *is* no one with an alternative viewpoint.

Consultation

 Taking account of what someone else thinks.

 Letting people feel they have expressed themselves.

> The Government has consulted Labour Party members on the proposal to increase the detention period for a terrorist suspect to 90 days, by asking them the following questions.
>
> • Do you think police should have the time to complete their investigations into suspected terrorists? (Yes / No / Not sure)
>
> • Do you think we should have new safeguards to protect innocent people? (Yes / No / Not sure)
>
> Letter to *The Independent*

Consultation, listening, service, choice, responsiveness – this is the fraudulent vocabulary of mediocracy.

The mediocratic intelligentsia knows the buzzwords of democratisation are hollow, but the fictions of openness and participation must be maintained. As long as things *appear* to be democratic, the relevant criteria will be satisfied.

Many people will not notice the discrepancy between image and reality, as they have been indoctrinated with the idea that ***appearance*** is all that matters. For those who do notice, the fraudulence can function as a demonstration that mediocracy is the sole arbiter of truth.

Cookery

☒ **Preparation of food for consumption.**

☑ **A significant art form.**

> The Food Studies Movement? We're right on the vanguard of it, in classic revolutionary terms. We're trying to establish food studies as a completely legitimate field of study, with very high standards, that people will take seriously.
>
> Marion Nestle, Professor of Food Studies

There are several ways in which high culture can be eradicated without simply abolishing it. One is to have an ersatz high culture that is so boring, vacuous and impenetrable that no one is tempted by it, except as a mediocratic career option.

Another way is to elevate pop culture to the position of high culture. This does not mean simply emphasising the popular, or saying it is equally good. Pop culture must be given the *deference* that high culture used to receive. Meanwhile, the original areas of high culture become increasingly repellent and marginalised, and it becomes fashionable to despise them.

Under mediocracy, the vocabulary of high culture becomes the vocabulary of pop culture. *Geniuses* are not artists or philosophers, but footballers and chefs.

Creativity

 Unusual talent possessed by exceptional individuals.

 Faculty possessed by all which (with training) can generate cultural output.

> All people are capable of creative achievement, provided the conditions are right and they have acquired the relevant skills. We favour a democratic conception of creativity: one which recognises the capacity for achievement in the many and not the few.
>
> Government report on creativity

The concept of the exceptional individual is incompatible with mediocratic ideology. To eliminate it, we must also eliminate a number of associated notions.

Ability, intelligence, genius, creativity: these things have to be redefined in a mediocracy. Preferably, they do not exist at all. Or if they do, they are shared equally by everyone – subject to first having received appropriate *training*.

Crisis

 Undesirable source of social instability.

 Essential prerequisite for desirable social change.

No state has been able to recast its society to the extent that Britain must do, without suffering defeat in war, economic collapse or revolution.

Will Hutton

Minor shifts or moderate improvements – these are forms of appeasement, designed to satisfy people's desire to believe that a wrenching transformation of society will not be necessary.

Al Gore

Mediocracy is essentially an ethos of stasis. However, it needs to wage constant war against those who might threaten this stasis. Paradoxically, the struggle to maintain stasis is aided by undermining stability. Chaos in the social realm is helpful; it is loss of control in the cultural realm which must be avoided.

Crisis is therefore welcomed and even invited. This explains an otherwise puzzling ambivalence towards those whom one might assume were enemies in the conventional sense, e.g. terrorists.

Mediocratic states are notably more enthusiastic in their treatment of crises than in their prevention. *Treatment* typically involves creating military havoc, restricting privacy and increasing regulation.

Culture

 The arts and other forms of intellectual achievement.

 A form of communal interaction which expresses social values.

> We define 'culture' as the shared values and patterns of behaviour that characterise different social groups and communities.
>
> Government report on creativity

> To complain about the arts in terms that take little note of the steady work being done by hundreds of thousands of decent, committed people across the country who would have had no place in the arts community fifty years ago – this is to speak false.
>
> Melvyn Bragg

Culture in a mediocracy is rebranded as an intrinsically social activity. Cultural output is to be regarded as an expression of the community rather than as the output of a few individuals.

Culture must always be seen as a product of its time and place, and determined by the position in *social space* (class, gender, etc.) of the individuals associated with its production.

The idea of an artist or intellectual standing outside the political process is bourgeois and hence invalid. Cultural output cannot, we are taught, be assessed or appreciated without awareness of its political motivations, social implications and historical context.

Degree

 Academic rank conferred on a person in respect of intellectual achievement.

 Certificate of training in basic maths, English and social interaction.

I graduated this summer in English from Warwick and ended the worst three years of my life. I had unfriendly lecturers and tedious lectures.

Tim Clist, *Independent*

Tim Clist is seeking to blame everyone but himself. Other students were producing films, running rock bands, working out, losing one faith and acquiring another, getting into debt and out again, vandalising GM crops, demonstrating against globalisation, hobnobbing with poets.

Professor Germaine Greer, Warwick University

A degree in a mediocracy is not something for the clever; it is something for everyone. There can be no place in a mediocratic society for activities targeted exclusively at the intelligent.

This means a degree should not be about intellectual development, but about something more socially oriented, such as experience of *diversity*.

Democracy

 The ability to choose between political parties with different philosophies.

 The right to treat politicians as ridiculous.

On Radio 4's *Woman's Hour*, Tory leadership candidates David Davis and David Cameron were asked what type of underpants they liked to wear, and whether they preferred blondes or brunettes.

BBC

After his failure in the 1992 election, Paddy Ashdown wrote in his diary, "What a terrible game, why do we do it?" Go on, Paddy, do please tell us. PLEASE. We want to know. Why do you do it?

Jeremy Paxman

The theory of democracy is that everyone's view is given equal weight. In practice, if no genuine alternatives are offered, the weight of each voter's view is zero. In a mediocracy, the political elite proceeds largely as it wishes, with the electorate's contribution limited to derision.

Some organisations in a mediocracy may have sufficient financial power to put the case for mildly dissenting viewpoints which, not surprisingly, tend to be biased towards a particular group of constituents (e.g. smokers). 'Making things more democratic' comes to mean 'eliminating the influence of such organisations', thus eliminating the only significant source of real diversity.

Democratisation

 Bringing something into line with mass opinion.

 Bringing mass opinion into line with what is deemed appropriate by the elite.

> The greatest trick is government-subsidised protest concerts like Live 8, where ministers are hand-in-glove with the celebrities to generate 'demands' for what ministers have already agreed.
>
> *Scotland on Sunday*

> When I studied Dickens, the way it was taught never related to the man in the street. It has got to.
>
> Sir Christopher Frayling, Chairman of the Arts Council

Democratisation is an example of mediocratic inversion. Although notionally referring to popularisation, or increasing accountability, in practice democratisation means making things more compatible with approved ideology.

The concept thus becomes a useful touchstone for abolishing things that an intelligent person might enjoy, without necessarily leading to any greater entertainment for anyone else. 'Democratised culture' is simply culture which the elite regards as suitable for the mass.

Depression

 Mental state resulting from bad life conditions, treatable by improvement in circumstances.

 Any state of unwellness not linked to a known disease, treatable with antidepressants.

> A term formerly restricted to those so severely afflicted that they might require hospitalisation has been adapted to cover a wide range of responses to distress, from workplace dissatisfaction to marital disharmony and bereavement.
>
> Michael FitzPatrick MD

A mediocracy relies on the suppression of criticism. Anomalous cases of dissatisfaction need to be identified as pathological. It is desirable to associate such anomalies with physiology, as this contributes support for *physicalism*.

Unhappiness should be presumed to be caused by a chemical deficiency or by incorrect thinking. It cannot be caused by dissatisfaction with, for example, the opportunities available for intellectuals. A mediocratic culture must be presumed to cater for all real (i.e. socially recognised) needs.

People expressing feelings of dissatisfaction should be regarded as requiring treatment. They should be strongly encouraged to take whichever drugs will cause them to stop complaining, whether these are drugs for happy feelings or – if necessary – drugs for no feelings at all.

Desperation

 Feeling of an individual who finds the state will not protect his territory.

 Feeling of an underprivileged person if the state does not offer him enough options.

> As long as young people feel they have got no hope but to blow themselves up, you are never going to make progress.
>
> Cherie Blair

Desperation is considered legitimate in a mediocracy only in those contexts where it can be used to justify hostility towards the bourgeoisie, business and similar targets.

In contexts where it represents frustration with being unable to rise above the mediocre, in a society obsessed with 'equality' and 'fairness', it is labelled pathological.

Dignity

 Something a person can have if his culture allows him to feel superior in some respect.

 Feeling of being no worse than anyone else, which the state must ensure all experience.

(1) Every employee shall have a right to dignity.

(2) An employer commits a breach if an employee suffers any conduct which causes him to be alarmed or distressed, including … unjustified criticism on more than one occasion … or changes in duties without reasonable justification.

Dignity at Work Bill

As in the case of *respect*, dignity is something a mediocracy must sound approving of, although in practice the phenomenon is incompatible with the mediocratic subordination of the individual to the group. A sense of dignity is too close to a sense of superiority, and no one should be allowed to feel superior to anyone else.

Diversity

 The presence of a variety of viewpoints, including those labelled 'conservative'.

 Permutations consistent with mass taste and egalitarian values.

> An apparent range of excitingly different styles will serve to disguise an underlying conformity of sentiment and vision. The real thing would be too scary.
>
> Tim Parks, novelist

An important inversion, since real diversity is not something that is compatible with mediocracy. The term is used principally to mean suppression of bourgeois culture.

Diversity is an example of the mediocratic phenomenon where a desired result can be achieved while pretending to aim at its opposite. In this case, *equality* (i.e. homogenisation) is achieved under cover of promoting plurality. A philosophy which supposedly seeks to promote cultural variety can be used to suppress work which seems insufficiently pro-egalitarian.

Doctor

 Person who provides medical services in accordance with a patient's wishes.

 Community agent who helps to ensure equal levels of health for all productive individuals.

The decision to withdraw artificial feeding from a patient is essentially one for the clinical judgement of responsible medical practitioners.

Judge Sir Stephen Brown, High Court

If people sue doctors, they are going to find their access to health care may be limited. That's a harsh thing to say, but this is a war.

Dr. John Jones, radiologist

Control over the body is an important component in mediocracy's control of society. It is therefore not allowed to remain in the hands of the individual.

A mediocratic doctor is employed to act in the best interests of the community, and to promote *justice*. If paid by the client, the service may be referred to as 'private medicine', but the doctor's duties to society are to remain binding.

As agents of the community, mediocratic doctors are presumed to be in the right. They may not be criticised except by another qualified professional. However, they should avoid criticising colleagues as this undermines professional solidarity. An increase in malpractice complaints should be blamed on excess individualism.

Dumbing down

 Lowering of standards resulting from egalitarian policies.

 Illustration of the evil effects of market forces.

In their book on inheritance tax, Professors Graetz and Shapiro identify Paris Hilton and Nicole Richie (stars of a TV show which sent the super-privileged pair out to encounter ordinary Americans with hilarious results) as poster-children for the absurd injustice of inherited wealth.

London Review of Books

Cultural crudification is regarded as desirable in a mediocracy, and not just because it expresses the prevailing ethos.

Dumbing down is one of a class of phenomena that can serve the objectives of mediocracy in two apparently opposite ways. On the one hand, it is promoted and celebrated, in order to displace bourgeois culture. On the other hand, it is condemned, and used to indict capitalism and individualism, by holding them responsible for it.

Economics

✗ **The study of commercial behaviour.**

✓ **Abstract mathematical modelling.**

PROPOSITION 3.1 Suppose the probabilities with which the game begins in each active state are given, and let B's strategy be fixed at the stationary and strictly positive value y. Then A's expected payoff is continuous in his strategy.

PROPOSITION 3.2 The model has a stationary perfect equilibrium. If the game is symmetric, then there exists a symmetric stationary perfect equilibrium.

PROPOSITION 3.3 Suppose that $P_A = P_B$ and $c_A = c_B$. Then symmetric equilibrium is unique if one of the following conditions holds:
(i) $c_A(z) = c_B(z) = z_\mu$ for some $\mu > 1$;
(ii) $N \le 3$ and Assumption C3 holds;
(iii) $N \le 5$, $c_A = c_B$ is twice continuously differentiable, and $c''_A = c''_B$ is monotonic non-decreasing.

Sir John Vickers and Professor Christopher Harris, analysis of R&D

Mediocratic economics provides an illustration of *academic theory*, which not only does not concern itself with reality but in some contexts *flaunts* its lack of concern as a signal of sophistication. An absence of meaningful content must be compensated for in some way; hence the high level of *technicality*, which also serves to emphasise that the activity is open only to the trained.

Economist

 Person able to analyse, and help others to understand, the workings of the economy.

 Trained expert who applies contemporary techniques of *economics* in approved ways.

> To the extent that anyone understands economics, they demonstrate the fact by using its terms and arranging them in an appropriate order.
>
> Professor Catherine Belsey, *Poststructuralism*

Economists in a mediocracy are not employed to increase understanding of the economy, but to generate output which will be classed as acceptable economics by their colleagues. We should therefore not be surprised if mediocratic economics fails to illuminate real phenomena, or is completely incomprehensible to those not versed in its terminology.

As with some other mediocratic high culture that is too egregious to escape comment, it may be permitted to opine that **economics** is unsatisfactory, provided one blames the usual acceptable targets: conservatism, markets, individualism.

The strange logic applied by pseudo-critiques of **economics** provides a good illustration of how alternative perspectives become impossible in mediocracy. In this case, it is argued that if a subject has become so obsessed with abstract mathematics that it clearly no longer refers to reality, it *can only be* because that subject reflects the vested interests of capitalism, or because it is not sufficiently concerned with social justice.

Education

 Imparting knowledge of facts.

Training in social skills and political awareness.

> The case for comprehensive schools is that it forces people to know each other who would otherwise have no relationships. A common education permits a redistribution downwards of cultural advantage.
>
> Dr. Ross McKibbin, Cambridge University

The concept of education is immensely appealing to mediocrats. It fits with the idea of the individual as a blank to be moulded into the appropriate outlook. However, education sometimes allows differences in ability to be expressed, and therefore also represents a threat.

Mediocratic education is controlled by the collective in order to reflect society's preferences. The *social* purposes of education turn out to be different from the private motives that led to it in the first place. They include absorbing as much of people's time as possible, and changing the objective from intellectual activity to ***inclusion***, i.e. exposure to the approved ideology.

Egalitarianism

 The belief that people of similar ability should have equal chances, regardless of background.

✓ **The belief that no economic inequality is justifiable.**

We are all egalitarians now. To deny basic human equality is to move beyond the pale of reasoned political debate.

Dr. John Tasioulas, Oxford University

We need to break down the false divisions based on class and envy that have been around for generations. They are wholly artificial. By 'classless society' I mean a society in which every promotion, every certificate is respected, and each person's contribution is valued.

Sir John Major

Appearances notwithstanding, mediocracy does not care about everyone having the same opportunities as those from favourable backgrounds. It would rather those opportunities did not exist at all. That is a much safer way of achieving equality of outcome.

Real opportunities provide scope for undesirable kinds of inequality, and are best avoided, or neutered to the point where they become unthreatening. Attending university, for example, must cease to be an experience available only to some. Attending a *famous* university must cease to be an experience that could in any way be described as *better* than that of attending other universities.

Elitism

 Unfairly excluding people because they do not subscribe to approved ideology or techniques.

 Unfairly excluding people because they are less able, or appear not to be interested.

> It is elitist to think that literature can only be appreciated by those with a particular sort of cultural breeding. Theory* is a way of emancipating literary works from this stranglehold, and throwing them open to a kind of analysis in which – in principle at least – anyone could participate.
>
> Professor Terry Eagleton

A mediocracy prides itself on being non-elitist. However, its real distinction lies in having a particular *kind* of elite. Entry to the mediocratic elite depends on accepting the rules of its game rather than on a particular level of ability. One must be able to *apply* the rules but it is not necessary to understand them.

Some basic rules are common to all areas of mediocratic culture.

- Make your subject appear open to all, while basing entry on ideological orientation and willingness to accept the rules.

- Jargon is essential for maintaining professional prestige.

- Output should be judged on presentation rather than content.

- Never state the rules explicitly.

---

* For an illustration of the accessibility of 'theory', see *Analysis*.

Equality

 An equal chance to compete.

 The promotion of under-represented social groups.

The terms 'comprehensive education' and 'equality of opportunity' are synonymous.

National Union of Teachers

In mediocracy, equality is not about opportunities for the able, but about something better called *homogeneity*. According to the axiom of homogeneity, human beings are essentially identical to one another, and reducible to simple mechanical interpretations. It follows there is no justification for unequal outcomes.

Homogeneity implies that no one should be different from anyone else in a way that might arouse resentment. Certainly not if the difference was acquired independently of the collective will, e.g. through the operation of the market, or by inheritance.

However, mediocracy does not actually result in equality of outcome, nor is it intended to. It is only certain kinds of inequality that are disliked, i.e. those which might generate autonomy for intellectuals. Other sorts can be condoned, or even promoted if the effect is to displace less acceptable kinds.

An economically advantaged individual who is sufficiently at the behest of others (e.g. a company director), or unlikely to do anything significant with his wealth (e.g. a lottery prize winner), does not represent a threat, and can therefore be tolerated.

Ethics

 Principles of behaviour based on respect for the individual.

 Rules consistent with egalitarianism.

> I don't think infanticide is always unjustifiable. People who think there is a difference between that and abortion have to ask: what happens to the foetus in the time it takes to pass down the birth canal? I don't think it is plausible that any moral change occurs. There is a very widespread and accepted practice of infanticide in most countries.
>
> John Harris, Professor of Bioethics

Only one thing is permitted to generate significant moral concern in a mediocracy: inequality. Other possible moral principles are conditional and subject to expediency. Respect for life or respect for privacy, for example, are not compatible with the mediocratic ethos. Our preconceptions in these areas must be dismantled, our emotional resistances worn away.

Ethical re-education is best achieved through culture rather than debate. Mediocratic fiction, for example, presents theft, murder and torture as amusing. Individual victims have no significance; they are mere ciphers. Only overall social goals matter, and those only to the extent that *equality* is at stake.

Evil

 Harsh treatment of vulnerable people in state institutions.

 Supply of addictive substances, except by doctors.

We will provide the resources for a database where every known offender will have their DNA recorded. What we said on new powers was attacked by civil liberties groups. I believe in civil liberties too: the liberty of young people not to die the victim of the most chilling, evil industry the world has to confront.

Tony Blair

Mediocratic ethics is simple. The only primary evils are (a) inequality, and (b) non-approved human desires. The latter category varies according to fashion but may include such diverse things as the profit motive, recreational drug use, and hostility towards other cultures.

Anything else is 'evil' only if it follows from either (a) or (b), leaving out such phenomena as child abuse by state agents, imprisoning of parents if their children do not attend school, breaking up of families on the authority of supposed experts, or horrible deaths from neglect in state hospitals. These are tolerated with relative equanimity since they are consequences of *social* rather than private weakness. A mediocracy may admit that state services are inefficient, but the *intentions* of state agents may not be questioned.

Examination

 Test of knowledge about a particular subject.

 Test to ascertain whether someone is able to employ the terminology of a subject.

> The examination system is above all a way of policing the profession, making sure that those who qualify to join it understand how its language or symbols are conventionally employed.
>
> Belsey, *Poststructuralism*

What matters in a mediocracy is not whether a person is able to carry on a productive activity, but whether they can conform to the appearance of doing so. Furthermore, it is crucial that cultural disciplines affirm rather than question the prevailing ideology. The criterion of what constitutes an accepted member of a profession is therefore redefined.

Appropriate entry to a mediocratic elite requires a filter that repels those who might previously have been admitted, while appearing still to be technically rigorous. Those who are interested in a subject for the wrong reasons, e.g. a desire to make progress, are threatening to the stability of mediocracy and must therefore be excluded.

The answer is (i) to devise abstruse techniques which can be used as indicators of professional expertise, but are so tedious as to alienate anyone with an interest in reality, and (ii) to make professional status depend on demonstrating facility with those techniques.

Excitement

 Emotional response to purposeful activity, or to entertainment based on narrative drama.

 Emotional response to observing extreme forms of violence, horror, criminality or sex.

These days, work has to be an advertisement for itself, otherwise people don't pay much attention. You've got a smaller audience if you don't do something shocking.

Richard Billingham, artist

I had to tell the studio for *Kill Bill*, "Don't worry about the blood, man. When the audience goes aaargh, they're having a good time. It's fun!" It's like I get you to reach climax with me about my own masturbatory fantasy.

Quentin Tarantino

One of the principal tasks for the mediocratic elite is how to manage people's emotions in an environment that has been stripped of all purpose and significance.

It is found that emotional energies are best rechannelled into politically innocuous activities such as sex, violence, physical danger, horror, or spectator sports. These can be enjoyed by way of participation, or by observing, either live or on screen.

Expert

 Person with specific knowledge who does not necessarily make better decisions than a layman.

 Authority figure who can only be criticised by other approved experts in the same field.

Angela Cannings, who spent 20 months in prison, has become the third woman in a year to have her conviction for murdering her babies, based on expert evidence from Sir Roy Meadows, overturned. The rash of cases has been blamed on an attitude of suspicion dating from when Home Office pathologist Professor Michael Green told colleagues to "think dirty" if babies were brought in who had died suddenly.

Daily Telegraph, 11 December 2003

Professionals must be able to undertake their duties without fear of ill informed attacks. There have been orchestrated campaigns to discredit expert opinion.

Professor Sir Alan Craft, 29 May 2004

In a mediocracy, truth means social consensus, and can therefore be determined only by authorised individuals who have received approved *training*. The position of 'expert' is conferred by the mediocratic elite on those who demonstrate commitment to the preferred viewpoints.

To contradict the opinion of an approved expert is to question the training, standards and benevolence of his profession. People who dare to do so should be treated with suspicion.

Fairness

 Treating people without ideological bias.

 The elimination of any inequality that has not been democratically sanctioned.

> Those who have been favoured by nature may gain from their good fortune only on terms that improve the situation of those who have lost out.
>
> Professor John Rawls

Is it fair that a relatively able person should end up with more freedom of action than one with less? According to mediocratic morality, no: such a person should end up with *less* freedom, as he is already benefiting from an unfair advantage.

Fairness and *equality* are the key moral notions of mediocracy. For example, 'fairness' is invoked to override contracts or other arrangements between individuals, if those arrangements conflict with mediocratic values. However, a mediocracy never becomes particularly equal or fair, even by its own supposed standards. This is partly because the measures taken to improve fairness usually involve the transfer of control from individuals to the state. Although the autonomy of some is reduced, that of the less fortunate is not necessarily increased.

In any case, mediocratic 'fairness' functions principally as a rhetorical device. Its primary purpose is not to remould society according to a particular distributional model, but to legitimise aggression against those at odds with mediocracy.

Feminism

 Philosophy which aims to remove institutional barriers for talented women.

 Ethic which insists on women as a group having an identical economic profile to men.

> Grrrl Power represents young women as angry and taking action. For example, Flea writes in her zine Thunderpussy, "Next time a bloke feels your arse or patronises you, forget the moral high ground. Just deck the bastard." I believe this attempt to reclaim power is worth looking at closely.
>
> Dr. Anita Harris, Monash University

Mediocracy is good at co-opting ideas that are pro-individual, and turning them into means for attacking individuals. Pre-mediocratic feminism demanded that women of high ability not be barred from competing with men. But individual women of high ability are not of concern to mediocratic feminists, any more than talented individuals from poor backgrounds are of concern to mediocratic egalitarians.

As with *egalitarianism*, the real objective is to have a justification for attacking some class of individual – in this case, men. It does not matter much who the targets for hostility are, but men are particularly suitable since in their pre-mediocratic manifestation they tended to be associated with qualities of which mediocracy disapproves, e.g. self-reliance, territoriality, competitiveness.

Freedom

 Having capital.

 Liberation from bourgeois ideology and capitalist power, achieved through education.

> Real freedom is unavailable to one whose horizons
> are so narrow that he can conceive only one way of
> life. An individual is only free by virtue of the whole
> society which brought him to be and nourishes him.
>
> Professor Charles Taylor, McGill University

To prevent anyone from arguing that freedom is restricted by mediocrity, it becomes necessary to redefine it.

Freedom is to be understood as the ability to make *correct* choices. Where a person makes choices that are in serious conflict with mediocratic values, it must be concluded that he is not truly free, in which case he may require suitable training to enable him to exercise mediocratic freedom.

Free speech

 The ability to express anti-egalitarian points of view.

 The principle that cultural producers should be able to present all aspects of reality, including suffering, viscera, torture, rape, etc.

People shouldn't think that the Index is against censorship on principle. It may have been so in its radical youth, but it is now as concerned with fighting hate speech as protecting free speech.

Associate Editor, Index on Censorship

The head of the Dermatology Department has strong feelings about exposure to sunlight. She felt that my recommendation to expose yourself for ten minutes a day was outside the realm of what she was teaching. She therefore asked me to resign.

Professor Michael Holick, Boston University

The idea of defending a principle such as free speech is incompatible with mediocracy, which has room for only one precept, *equality*. Other principles are dismissed, unless they can be demonstrated to have obvious usefulness for the majority.

If enough people find an idea objectionable, a mediocracy will either make it unlawful to express it, or simply cease protecting those who do express it from the criminal acts of others. Blasphemy against the doctrine of equality is particularly liable to fall foul of mediocratic tolerance. So is arguing with the views of doctors or other approved experts, or questioning their motives.

Fun

 Light-hearted entertainment or pleasure.

 Activities which amuse by making someone feel despised or inadequate.

> In *Reservoir Dogs*, the character Mr. Blonde tells the captive cop, after beating him, cutting him with a razor, and before slicing off his ear and dousing him with gasoline, "Nobody tells me what to do. It's amusing to me to torture."
>
> *Journal of Popular Film and Television*

Mediocracy advertises itself as valuing respect, empathy and consideration. The content of its entertainments indicates a different ethos. TV show contestants are bullied, insulted and humiliated. Characters in literature and drama are abused, tortured and mutilated.

Given a model of the human being as a degraded and insignificant entity, it is not surprising that mediocratic fun often expresses contempt for the individual. "We (society, the group, the audience) are dominant; you are insignificant and in our power" is the underlying message.

Genius

 Individual with exceptionally high degree of intelligence and/or creativity.

 Historical figure who was highly productive as a result of unfair advantages.

 Famous dead footballer or comedian.

> The commonsense view of invention overstates the importance of geniuses. The answer to the question, would the pattern of world history have been altered significantly if some genius inventor had not been born, is clear: there has never been any such person.
>
> Jared Diamond

History, as taught prior to mediocracy, is replete with apparently exceptional individuals. Mediocracy regards this as regrettable, and looks for acceptable ways to account for it.

Perhaps, it argues, it is due to the biased perspective of bourgeois culture, which seeks out individuals who can function as heroes in a satisfying narrative. Or it is a result of the extreme inequalities which were a feature of early capitalism. Either way, the concept of genius becomes suspect, although it may continue to be used in areas that are considered sufficiently unthreatening, such as sports.

Gifted

 Unusually able, needing to be allowed to be precocious.

 Maladapted, requiring social support.

According to Margaret Sutherland of Glasgow University, gifted pupils are not being allowed to fail, and this has emotional consequences. "To be constantly told that you have done well means these children are not challenged."

BBC News

We recommend moving away from the term 'gifted', because of its suggestion of exclusiveness and narrow scope. The recommended alternative term is 'very able, with specific gifts and talents', to be shortened for ease of use to 'very able'.

Director of Education, Wirral Council

Potential innovators are dangerous to mediocracy. They are unpredictable. They may generate cultural output which conflicts with mediocratic values. It is safer not to encourage belief in such persons, and to avoid such concepts as 'gifted' or 'genius'. The status of 'innovator' should depend exclusively on promotion by the collective.

As a supplementary strategy, it is possible to make achievement-oriented individuals appear suitably unattractive by assessing them in terms of mediocratic values. In fiction, aspirant geniuses should be presented as maladapted or malevolent, preferably both.

Government

 Necessary evil, required in certain narrowly defined areas.

 The fount of all morality.

> The health of the family and the strength of the nation ultimately reflect the quality of honest, decent, truthful government – government which has a moral dimension and which always makes sure that justice has a high place at the Cabinet table.
>
> Tony Blair

> I am surprised that many are instinctively suspicious of the state and insist on their absolute protection against it. The state can be a positive force, empowering people to shape their lives, a collective vehicle to achieve progressive change.
>
> David Blunkett, Home Secretary

In mediocracy, government is portrayed as the benevolent representative of the community. This model is important, because it supports the claim that transfers of economic power from private individuals to the state represent increases in equality and hence are ethically desirable.

The possibility that the government generates activity which does not benefit anyone, other than perhaps those directly employed by it, is considered irrelevant to the question of whether it is a force for good. Government embodies *public* rather than private values, and as such is to be regarded as morally superior to markets.

Group

✗ **Collection of people.**

✓ **Benevolent social formation which turns
selfish individuals into caring cooperators.**

> Consultants helping an executive to organise a staff
> meeting announced that the company would first
> need to have a thorough cultural audit. Having
> carried out the audit, they advised that the meeting
> should include a "celebration of each individual as an
> important member of the team", and that the best way
> of achieving this would be a group hug.
>
> *Financial Times*

Mediocracy promotes group activity in all areas of life, with
the emphasis on interactions with *strangers*. Other types of
relation are considered less helpful, as they may generate loyalties
that run counter to the interests of society. The formation of small
private self-selected groups such as families, minority sects or small
businesses is therefore discouraged in favour of massive state schools,
religions with a large constituency, and mega-corporations.

Institutional education is useful for promoting a group ethic. Mediocracy therefore extends the model of education beyond its traditional
boundaries, bringing more age groups and more hours of the day
under its jurisdiction. Mediocratic schools organise extracurricular
activities, with the implicit message that to exclude your child from
them will be regarded as antisocial.

Hegemony

 Dominance of *liberal* outlook in academia, journalism, education, the arts, etc.

 Dominance of capitalism, and of bourgeois cultural concepts, in Western societies.

> Whenever some bullet-headed Conservative minister wants to characterise a bad teaching method, he attaches the word 'trendy' to the practice, without pausing to consider that it is all the simplistic ideas of the Right which have been so markedly à la mode.
>
> Sir David Hare

> My teachers said we must not help 'class enemies'. But I did not know who they were, and my teachers were not keen to elaborate.
>
> Jung Chang, *Wild Swans*

Mediocracy needs to maintain the fiction that rival ideologies represent a serious threat, and that the fight against them can never cease. The smallest sign of opposition is magnified to suggest that the old enemy is still powerful.

It can never be admitted that it is mediocratic ideology which is dominant, since that would undermine its attraction of being supposedly non-conformist and avant-garde.

Hero

 Idealistic individual who fights against the odds for an impersonal cause.

 Clever criminal.

 Brutish male who engages in physical combat in order to rescue a female and have sex with her, and/or to cause the painful death of one or more members of the bourgeoisie.

'Heroes of History: Guy Fawkes'

Channel 5 television programme

Mediocracy hates the idea of a hero. An exceptional individual? Who decides on his own course of action, independently of the social consensus? Without first consulting a committee of experts?

There can be no heroes in the present. That would be inconsistent with the mediocratic model of the *individual*.

With regard to the past, figures that were previously identified as heroes need to be rebranded. Their unheroic aspects (sexual idiosyncrasies, personality defects) need to be emphasised – or invented. They need to be made to appear as proletarian as possible or, if this proves difficult, they should be discredited for being anti-egalitarian.

High culture

 Cultural output which draws on higher brain functions, intended to enlighten or inspire.

 Whatever is designated by a trained practitioner as 'art', 'philosophy', etc.

Creators are motivators of political and social change. The creative world is not there to make anyone feel warm and cosy; it is there to ask, to probe, to challenge, and to be awkward. That in itself is a fine social purpose.

Chris Smith, Minister for Culture

The mediocratic elite determines who shall be allowed to be active in areas regarded as high culture. What kind of people are appointed to the role of cultural producer? Those whose work is most likely to reinforce mediocratic values.

A keenness to work within prescribed structures is a desirable characteristic for a producer. So is an interest in abstruse technique. A certain kind of aggression or rebelliousness can be valuable if aimed against non-mediocratic values, e.g. romanticism or privacy.

An interest in reality, on the other hand, is an undesirable characteristic, since it is likely to lead to activity which subverts rather than reinforces the mediocratic ethos. Interest in reality conflicts with the preferred approach of consulting the social consensus, and presumes that there *is* a reality independent of social agreement. It could also undermine the validity of existing mediocratic output that is technically proficient but vacuous.

Ideology

 Philosophies which are pro-egalitarian.

 Attitudes supportive of capitalism.

> The phrase 'freedom-loving' is rich with ideology. It is an imaginary representation of a nation as a crusader for freedoms, and serves to promote the economic interests of that nation.
>
> Professor Michael Freeden, Oxford University

The term *ideology* usually means: a philosophy which functions as a political tool rather than as a means to understanding the world, and which is therefore to be viewed critically.

Mediocratic culture is driven by a political agenda. However, a mediocracy cannot admit to having an ideology, since this would imply that its vision was not as authoritative or objective as it wants people to think.

The best form of defence is attack. Anything anti-mediocratic is therefore identified as *ideological,* using mediocratic techniques of *analysis* – which are ideal for this purpose. Having done this hard enough and long enough, a stage is reached where 'ideology' comes to mean, simply, *anti-mediocracy.*

Inclusion

 Ensuring all citizens have access to bourgeois culture.

 Ensuring all citizens are acquainted with contemporary ideology.

> Despite the inclusion statements in the National Curriculum, equality is still not at its heart. The National Curriculum does not facilitate the preparation of pupils for adult life in a diverse society. Neither [sic] does it encourage the meeting of specific needs such as those of minority ethnic pupils and those from deprived backgrounds.
>
> National Union of Teachers

On the face of it, mediocrats have great interest in marginalised social groups – e.g. other races, other sexualities, the disabled. This is presented as driven by compassion and a desire for fairness. There are, however, other motivations at work. In mediocracy it is not individuals that matter but groups or *communities*. The characteristics and 'needs' of each community, and its place within the ideological framework, are determined by mediocratic experts.

Once defined and characterised, minority groups become concepts that serve a specific political function. They are used to legitimise hostility towards the bourgeoisie. Aggression against bourgeois individuals is rationalised by reference to concern for non-bourgeois groups. However, in practice non-bourgeois *individuals* are of little interest to mediocrats, particularly if they do not conform to the approved model of their group.

Indifference

> The problem for much of today's intelligentsia is not dumbing down, it is lack of proportion. They are like spoilt children who do not know how lucky they are.
>
> David Goodhart, Editor of *Prospect*

The well-adjusted individual in a mediocracy does not concern himself with the question of whether the changes that are happening around him are desirable. He is sufficiently mature and sophisticated to appreciate that the people in power are trained experts, who know more about the relevant issues than he does.

To question change is futile and obstructionist. Change is intrinsically desirable, since it represents **progress**. The modern world is dynamic and fast moving, and the old rules do not apply.

Certain phenomena, which might once have been experienced as alarming, need to be seen as inevitable signs of modernisation. These include such things as lying by officials, dumbing down, dismantling of civil liberties, increasing aggression, and the redefinition of terms and concepts.

Individual (normal)

 Product of own ideas and drives.

✓ **Product of biological and social forces.**

> We accept as a truism that people are importantly the
> product of their environment.
>
> Professor Michael Freeden

> The new needs of the contemporary sane person
> are organised around the fact that he lives as if he is
> exactly the same as everyone else, and totally different
> at the same time.
>
> Adam Phillips

In mediocracy, the concept of the individual is that of a physiological mechanism programmed to satisfy low grade impulses such as sex and aggression. Notions such as self, consciousness and free will are considered delusions that must be corrected by education.

The mediocratic individual has no autonomous inner world, i.e. one that is free from being determined by biological and social factors. His choices, while possibly unpredictable in detail, are ultimately trivial. He has no emotions beyond those implanted and sanctioned by society. He is a sink for everything, and a source of nothing.

But that is just the kind of individual that is wanted in a mediocracy. A person who is no threat to its systems, who subordinates himself to its authority figures, and who can be relied on to uphold its beliefs without question.

Individual (exceptional)

 Highly talented person, source of cultural innovation.

 Antisocial individual, driven by dubious motives, often responsible for evil.

> Guy Gibson, leader of the World War 2 dam-busters, was pompous, conceited, and generally disliked … a humourless, self-important loner unable to relate to others … a compulsive womaniser, scarcely able to help himself from propositioning any female he met.
>
> Sir Max Hastings

In a mediocratic society, exceptionality becomes something presumed to be bad rather than good. Sanity is defined in terms of the average, and deviation from the average has to be explained by reference to some kind of pathology. It is taught that individuals who have been inadequately socialised, or who are psychologically unusual, are likely to become serial murderers, sexual perverts, or otherwise sociopathic.

It is also taught that the evil acts of societies are typically the result of aberrant individuals driven by excessive egotism. The atrocities committed under repressive regimes are to be identified with the figureheads of those regimes. Other agents involved were simply misled; in the absence of the evil leader, the atrocities would not have happened.

Individualism

✘ **Belief in the virtue of self-reliance.**

✘ **Belief in respect for other individuals.**

✘ **Belief that each individual is innately unique.**

People don't have interests that they carry around independent of social context. When we say professors have an 'interest' in teaching, or research, we are saying that to function in the role of 'professor', they have to define certain situations as calling for certain actions.

Professor Alexander Wendt

Mediocracy portrays the individual as degraded, and little more than the passive product of external forces. In spite of this model, mediocracy is said to be characterised by *individualism*. Although the original concept referred to self-reliance, and opposition to collectivism, these characteristics are not considered relevant to the mediocratic definition. In mediocracy, 'individualism' means uninhibited behaviour rather than respect for individuals. Hence increases in violence and crime are, paradoxically, interpreted as evidence of excess individualism.

The fact that there may be *more options*, as a result of economic growth, is confused with the issue of whether there is *more respect* for individual choice within the options available. Thus greater spending power for the *mass* is taken to signify that a mediocracy is

Belief in the importance of clothing choices.

 Belief in the disinhibition of aggressive impulses.

 Freedom to express oneself in the same way as everyone else.

> In today's world, we have unprecedented opportunities to create our own identities. The social world confronts us with a dizzying array of choices. The decisions we take – about what to wear, how to behave and how to spend our time – help to make us who we are.
>
> Anthony Giddens

becoming more 'individualistic', even as the government increasingly regulates and restricts personal behaviour such as childcare or food consumption.

Many practices described as 'individualistic' are nothing the individuals affected have chosen, but a form of anarchism delivered from above. For example, education in which students are left to their own devices, at the behest of educators; or intervention to 'help' people, applied coercively. Encouraging people to rebel against employers, parents or spouses is presented as being pro-individual, but in practice promotes destructiveness towards other individuals.

Indoctrination

 Promoting hostility to capitalism, the middle class, or the culture of 'dead white males'.

 Promoting bourgeois values.

> The traditional museum should be contrasted with a modern one that sends clear interpretative messages. Museum experience must be a trigger for social and ethical discourse. Museum design today is about transmitting learning in a shared social experience.
>
> Ralph Appelbaum, museum designer

Mediocratic culture contains a number of *myths* designed to deflect attention from its own shortcomings. Often the myth consists of an inversion, e.g. the idea that bourgeois culture is suffused with ideology that supports capitalism, but that mediocracy itself is free of ideological bias.

Another important myth is that a capitalist society *indoctrinates* its citizens with bourgeois values, while mediocracy heroically rescues us from indoctrination by ensuring that education and culture are characterised by 'analysis', 'challenge' and so on.

In reality, indoctrination is practised freely and intensively by mediocracy. A mediocracy believes harder in the correctness of its values than any capitalist or imperialist society. Mediocratic schools and universities regard it as a fundamental goal to impart mediocratic values, e.g. *fairness*.

Journal

 Publication which disseminates academic research to a wider audience.

 Publication which proves that an academic's work has been approved by his colleagues.

In a 1982 study, twelve articles from a range of psychology journals were resubmitted under new names to the same journals. Only three were recognised as resubmissions. Of the other nine, eight were rejected by the journals that had already published them, the most frequent ground for rejection being 'serious methodological flaws'.

Nelson & Watt, *Academic Keywords*

Mediocratic high culture is driven by ideology, relies on dubious techniques, and involves misrepresentations of reality. It therefore does not stand up well to critique. Hence dissenters must not be given a platform for criticism. In the arts, this can be difficult, since there is a market, as well as a professional elite. Orchestral music that is painful rather than enjoyable may receive professional approval, but is unlikely to fill concert halls.

In *academia*, on the other hand, there is no corresponding market. It is therefore relatively straightforward to exclude the wrong kinds of economist, physicist, philosopher, etc. The key instrument of exclusion is the *journal*, which works as follows.

1) No one is permitted to be an academic unless they publish articles in approved journals at a sufficient rate.

2) Articles are accepted by journals only if their approach and conclusions match current intellectual fashion.

Justice

 The protection of personal and property rights.

✓ **The elimination of inequality.**

> Young people from the top three social classes are almost three times as likely to enter higher education as those from the bottom three. This state of affairs cannot be tolerated in a civilised society. It is inherently socially unjust.
>
> White Paper on higher education

The following are possible forms of injustice. A rich person has their car stolen by someone from a poor background; someone accused of a crime is presumed guilty until proven innocent; university applicants are rejected because they attended private schools.

Here are some other phenomena that have been labelled unjust: the poor have a shorter life expectancy than the rich; some people express hostile opinions about religious groups; less than half of company directors are women.

Whether a society is biased against the first or the second group in defining justice usually indicates its position on the bourgeois versus mediocratic spectrum. It would be a mistake, however, to think that a mediocracy *cares* about injustices of the second type. Emotional interest is corralled towards the second class; this is done in order to divert attention from the first. The point is to legitimise persecution of the bourgeoisie, not to generate a desirable outcome for any individual.

Killing

 Causing the death of an individual; unacceptable except in war or self-defence.

 Legitimate destruction of an ill person for his own good, or of an antisocial person for the good of his community.

> The Amazon tribe's murder of the white anthropologist was not a mindless killing, but done on behalf of the community.
>
> BBC documentary

> A depressed mother who killed her Down's Syndrome son has been given a suspended jail sentence. The unbearable pressure Wendolyn Markcrow had been under made his "merciful sentence" the right one, the judge said.
>
> BBC News

Mediocratic ethics is focused on groups, not individuals. For example, war (involving attacks on whole groups) becomes marginally less acceptable under mediocracy, but involuntary euthanasia (killing individuals) becomes more acceptable.

The traditional objection to murder, based on the sanctity of the individual, is considered old-fashioned. It places too much emphasis on the value of a single person, and assumes that an individual is a discrete and permanent entity – an assumption that mediocratic academics labour to expose as erroneous.

Language

 Means for individuals to convey their thoughts to one another.

✓ **The origin and foundation of all mental phenomena.**

Language actively constructs the self.

Understanding the Self, Open University

The person is the subject of a sentence, and the figure that says 'I'. But at the same time the subject is *subjected* to the meanings and sentence structures that language permits. It follows that the subject is condemned to citationality.

Belsey, *Poststructuralism*

Language is social, and all knowledge has to be expressed using some kind of language. This makes it easy to claim that everything, including reality, depends on language, and hence on social agreement. A procession of intellectual movements have argued in favour of this proposition – semiologists, structuralists, poststructuralists, linguistic philosophers, critical theorists, etc. The received view of mediocracy is that their findings should be regarded as self-evident.

The linguistic approach to reality is a key component in the portrayal of truth as social rather than objective. It is therefore to be regarded as sacrosanct.

Law

 System defining what is prohibited, giving certain rights to those accused of breach.

 Mechanism which should be used in whatever way will generate the preferred result.

Anyone acquitted of a serious crime can now be brought back to trial in cases where 'new' evidence is found. The Attorney-General Peter Goldsmith explained that if the change did not go through, he would not be able to look murder victim Julie Hogg's mother in the eye.

Helena Kennedy QC

Violations of established legal principles in Nazi Germany included the replacement of 'formal wrongdoing' with the idea that every violation against community goals is wrong *per se*.

Burleigh, *The Third Reich*

Old-fashioned law did too much to protect individuals from the social will. The mediocratic model avoids bourgeois notions such as *principles* or *liberties*. If the community believes someone should be punished, the legal system should not put obstacles in the way. The idea of providing protection for defendants from the state is no longer required, as modern state agents can be presumed to act on behalf of *society* rather than on behalf of an elite.

Mediocracy believes in having as many laws as possible, but enforcing them selectively. This provides maximum flexibility, since harassment can be targeted at appropriate individuals.

Legitimisation

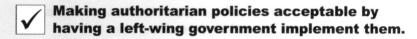
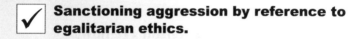
> Look at the picture of Americans running from the 9/11 explosions. American bond traders, you may say, are as undeserving of terror as Vietnamese peasants. Well, yes and no. America has democracy; if it often seems a greedy and overweening power, that is partly because its people have willed it.
>
> *New Statesman* editorial

A key aim of mediocracy is to make certain kinds of aggression morally acceptable, i.e. those aimed at the non-mediocratic. Aggression which undermines family and other private relationships is considered desirable, as is aggression targeted at the middle class, who must be punished for having more liberty than is consistent with egalitarianism.

Legitimisation involves generating mythologies which portray the bourgeoisie as aggressors. The more that white middle class males, for example, can be regarded as abusers, rapists or exploiters, the more it becomes acceptable for others to insult, rob or kill them.

Laws and policies which in other contexts might be regarded as oppressive – censorship, discrimination, abolition of liberties – are tolerated if the supposed motive is to increase *fairness*, i.e. to penalise the bourgeoisie.

Liberal

✗ **Person in favour of liberty.**

✓ **Privileged person who supports state-enforced social *justice* for other people.**

> David Hare has managed to remain a critic of society and a scourge of hypocrisy while acquiring a title, a house in Hampstead, and marriage to the independently famous Nicole Farhi.
>
> *Guardian*

> If it's the last thing I do, I'm going to destroy every f***ing grammar school in Britain.
>
> Privately educated Labour Minister Tony Crosland, 1965

In a mediocracy, the term 'liberal' no longer has anything to do with freedom. What a mediocratic liberal is liberal towards is confiscation of income and capital to finance the public sector.

Mediocratic liberals dislike 'conservatives', i.e. people who do not favour increases in state intervention. They denounce them as immoral, and may lash out at them with ferocity. Mediocratic liberals regard their own beliefs as admirable, and treat them as if they constituted a religion.

Mediocratic liberals can get emotional about what they regard as injustices. They are not usually victims themselves of these injustices, but may get angry on behalf of groups they regard as oppressed. They typically do not number members of any of these groups among their friends and acquaintances.

Liberty

 Freedom from oppressive restriction by the state.

 Spurious concept invoked by capitalists to justify less *welfare*.

> If intimidated juries have to be replaced by a judge sitting alone, it will not be an act of sabotage on civil liberties, it will be providing liberty and freedom for all the rest of us who have to put up with criminal actions day in and day out.
>
> David Blunkett, Home Secretary

The mediocratic recipe for abolishing liberty is as follows. *First*, introduce additional, spurious liberties such as the right not to be deported if you are an illegal immigrant, or the right of thieves to sue homeowners who injure them. Leave to simmer.

Second, discover that these liberties make it impossible to protect people from crime.

Third, announce that liberty has got out of hand and will have to be restricted in the interests of the community.

Fourth, exploit the new anti-libertarian climate to abolish the original liberties that existed before the introduction of the new ones.

Literacy

 Knowledge of a subject; the ability to read and write.

 Ability to use a subject in everyday life, especially in a way that supports egalitarian values.

> Mathematical literacy is defined as the capacity to identify, understand and engage in mathematics, and to make well-founded judgements about the role that mathematics plays in an individual's private life, occupational life, social life with peers and relatives, and life as a constructive, concerned and reflective citizen.
>
> OECD Report on education

The concept of literacy provides a good illustration of the mediocratic approach to intellectual activity. The old bourgeois version of literacy is rejected as too mechanical and tedious. The updated concept is advertised as simpler, and free from learning pointless techniques. However, the new techniques introduced are actually more arcane and ideological than anything generated by the older version.

This approach is duplicated in other subject areas. In theory, there is a shift from (a) learning *stuff*, to (b) learning how to learn, learning general principles, learning how to communicate, etc.

In practice, the shift is from learning old stuff (information) to learning new stuff (jargon, technique, ideology). The point is not to make things easier for learners, but to replace content with *technicality*.

Literature

 Written works intended to stimulate thought or imagination.

 Written works which generate social awareness or encourage political engagement.

Is literature a set of stories that seduce readers into accepting the hierarchical arrangements of society? Or is it the place where ideology is exposed, revealed as something that can be questioned?

Professor Jonathan Culler, Cornell University

Comrade Stalin has called our writers of literature "engineers of human souls". This means the truthfulness and historical concreteness of their artistic portrayal should be combined with ideological remoulding and education.

Andrei Zhdanov, Soviet Writers Congress 1934

Mediocratic literature, like mediocratic art, exists to convey a certain ideology and a certain world view.

Politically, we get the expected messages: capitalism is ruthless, the bourgeoisie is beastly, the West exploits the developing world.

Aesthetically, mediocratic writing purveys a grim landscape of decline, of physicality (sex, physiology, disease), of degraded characters lacking meaningful psychology. This becomes known as *realism*, although the version of reality presented is no less slanted than that of any other literature.

Lying

 Stating a falsehood intended to mislead; generally considered unacceptable.

 Using selectivity or devices when reporting; acceptable if done for socially desirable ends.

> The Labour Party kept files called 'real people' – lists of seemingly ordinary individuals who could be called upon at a moment's notice to endorse Labour in public, or to pose for photoshoots. And if too few 'real people' were around, party workers would make up the numbers.
>
> Former Labour election campaign officer

There are a number of reasons why truthfulness is not considered necessary in a mediocracy.

- Mediocratic analysis casts doubt on whether concepts such as objectivity are meaningful.

- Mediocratic techniques such as **blurring** and **boggling** create the impression that reality is fuzzy.

- Appropriate social ends are assumed to justify any means.

- The primary audience for mediocratic output is the mass, not the intelligentsia, and the mass is presumed to be less interested in whether something is true than in whether it holds the attention.

Majority rule

 System of least evil, whereby the worst misuses of power can sometimes be avoided.

 Principle that the welfare of a large number justifies any level of harm to an individual.

> Professor of Bioethics Peter Singer poses himself the question: would he torture to death an innocent child if by doing so he would secure happiness for the rest of mankind? Singer says yes.
>
> *Financial Times*

Democracy is to be regarded as much more than merely a form of government that claims the lowest risk of abuse. As it is consistent with the principle of *equality* (i.e. that everyone has identical rights and claims), it becomes a moral precept applicable to every area of life.

This approach is astute, as it can be used to legitimise attacks on individuals, especially if majority opinion can be manipulated in appropriate directions. Such manipulation is relatively easy in a mediocracy, since *education* has been designed to make the mass uncritical of social authority.

Management

 Running an organisation.

 The development of strategies to harness the maximum potential of employees, by providing a vision that evokes passion and hence empowering staff to become more creative.

Do your managers wear their passion on their sleeves? Is 'we care' your implicit motto? In an age of Creation Intensification the boss's mantra (is he a *boss*?) is: "Please commit your heart and soul to inventing wonderful solutions-experiences-dreams come true."

Tom Peters

Railtrack's Great Western Zone had been declining for at least a decade prior to the crash. This had resulted in lots of meetings and discussions, but not much action.

Paddington train crash Inquiry

Mediocratic management is not about providing what end users want in as trouble-free a way as possible. It is about generating a culture that celebrates corporate values and in which employees can feel included. It involves more training, more meetings and more assessment than older versions.

Mediocratic management is a sophisticated discipline which requires prior college training. It is not considered appropriate to learn it 'on the job'.

Market

 Method people use to exchange things.

 Harsh mechanism designed to exploit people's needs and satisfy selfish desires.

The unholy market kills the divine life of the mind.*

Times Higher Education Supplement

Art is being treated as a commodity. Perhaps capitalism will absorb it to the point of neutrality.

Jeanette Winterson OBE

We should expect mediocracy to be hostile to markets. Markets are the result of individual decisions and not – at least in their pure form – controlled by society. It is markets which allow individuals to accumulate capital and achieve independence from the collective.

In a mediocracy any undesirable phenomenon where money changes hands, or a business is involved, is blamed reflexively on 'markets', in spite of the fact that the same phenomenon could equally well have taken place in a planned economy.

Experiments involving the abolition of markets proved unworkable. It is now realised that a better way to create sustainable mediocracy is not to abolish markets but to manipulate them. Confiscating half the national product and dissipating it in useless ways, particularly in the form of wages to state employees providing spurious ***services***,

---

* Headline of an article about *government* demands that academic research should have useful outcomes.

118

is a good way to eliminate the larger part of the potential freedom that markets create.

Biasing confiscation towards the better off helps to ensure that the market reflects the preferences of the *mass*. One result is that those most likely to achieve economic freedom are those least likely to use it in culturally significant ways, e.g. footballers, movie stars, providers of cheap goods.

The mediocratic market for culture reveals the economic power of the *mass*. Tickets to pop concerts, for example, cost far more than those for classical music. It is, however, important to maintain the fiction that a small privileged class, purchasing elitist commodities such as opera, antiques or country estates, controls culture. This legitimises the continuation of the class war.

Notwithstanding mediocratic claims to the contrary, culture has always been subject to market forces. Cultural markets embody the values of those with spending power. They are compatible either with genuine content, or with superficiality. The conditions of mediocracy ensure that its markets tend to generate the latter.

If cultural output dumbs down, this can be blamed on 'the market', rather than on those who represent the bulk of cultural consumption, or on the policies which inflate their economic power. Markets thus function as a useful scapegoat for cultural deterioration. This is part of the reason why mediocracy finds it expedient to retain them.

Market economy

 System in which there is no state intervention in the exchange of goods and services.

 Markets for goods, state control of key services, and a tax rate of around 50%.

> The market economy is not an act of nature; it is socially produced and politically governed. Free markets do not of themselves produce the 'best' institutions and outcomes; they must be carefully sustained by social and public action.
>
> Will Hutton

Mediocracy does not want people to think that markets are what emerge if you let people act without interference. That makes them seem too attractively libertarian.

It is better to promote the idea that they are *social constructs*, and hence reflect particular class interests, and particular ideologies.

The idea that *opposition* to markets – or feigned opposition – may reflect the interests of a cultural elite is carefully avoided.

'Masculine'

 Territorial, responsible, objective, adventurous.

 Interested in football, drinking and sex, with tendencies to oppression, violence and rape.

Males are theorised to value autonomy, which is thought to depend on a highly individuated concept of persons. Highly individuated selves are seen as incapable of trust-based human attachments, unresponsive to human needs, and thriving on separation and competition.

Professor Marilyn Friedman

Although mediocracy is broadly hostile to maleness as being too individualistic, it is relatively tolerant of the proletarian version. Aggression, crude sexuality and yobbishness may be notionally criticised by mediocrats, but in practice they are condoned because they are compatible with the mediocratic ethos. The type of masculinity disapproved of more is that which believes in private rather than community rights, in individual responsibility rather than state support, and which does not think the self should be subordinate to the group.

With the traditional markers of maleness – responsibility, heroism, status – dismissed or belittled, the principal criterion of masculinity becomes sexual achievement, and the principal source of shame lack of sexual proficiency.

The mass

 The working class.

✓ **The people with money for luxuries.**

> Madison Avenue has coined a phrase to describe the
> latest marketing technique – 'masstige' or prestige
> for the masses. Today, luxury brands increasingly are
> within reach of anyone.
>
> *Business Week*

Aspects of mediocracy appear to reflect the preferences of the mass. There is more pop than classical, more soaps than theatre, more media studies than mathematics. Mediocracy loves ordinariness and things that bring everyone down to the same level. It is therefore tempting to regard it as a form of democratisation.

However, mediocracy is not about empowering the mass but about disempowering the individual. Mass taste is to be exploited in so far as it contributes to the agenda of degradation: encouraged where it does so, discouraged where it does not.

For example, the mass normally has little interest in high culture and can be invoked to condemn such culture where this is politically expedient. On the other hand, the mass is not entirely to be trusted since its instincts are not always mediocratic. It may have aspirations and a wish to better itself. Also, the mass is liable to be sceptical about the intellectual pretensions on which mediocratic ideology depends.

The key to exploiting the mass is to stimulate and satisfy its lowbrow impulses, while repelling its interest in anything more purposeful or sophisticated. There may be superficial efforts to entice the mass into the temples of high culture, but the content of these attempts is carefully selected so that there are no perceptible advantages over popular culture, and no risk that anyone outside the elite will be seriously tempted by it.

Creators of mediocratic high culture can consider themselves above the mass, which cannot be expected to understand their work – although it must nevertheless be produced for the mass's 'benefit'. Academia and the arts are therefore effectively immune from lay criticism, and authorised practitioners can publish more or less anything, provided it demonstrates sufficient awareness of fashionable techniques and references to gain the approval of their peer groups.

Meaning

 That aspect of culture which makes it interesting.

 Problematic concept, best avoided.

Otherness lays all oppositions open to deconstruction, leaving no pure concepts that can be taken as foundational. Meanings, not only the meaning of 'art' but of 'democracy' itself, are not given in nature or guaranteed by any existing authority.

Belsey, *Poststructuralism*

It is Byzantine to treat theoretical questions as if they had a value in themselves. Ideas are a continually renewed expression of historical development.

Antonio Gramsci

By means of **boggling** and other pseudo-sceptical techniques, mediocracy undermines the idea that things are capable of having a definite meaning. This is sometimes presented as being libertarian and pro-individualistic. In fact, the opposite is true.

Meaning, in its original sense, belongs to a class of concepts which can be invoked in potential opposition to the collective. If we cannot appeal to ideas such as meaning or objectivity, we simply fall back on social consensus as the criterion of reality – which is precisely the intention.

Meritocracy

 System of ranking individuals by means of objective standards, e.g. exam performance.

 Selection on the basis of social skills, or on the basis of moral merit.

> Everyone agrees that applicants should be selected on merit, the problem is defining it. Merit could mean admitting applicants with the highest marks in examinations, or it could mean taking into account context, background and relevant skills.
>
> Schwartz Report on higher education

> The new egalitarianism is sceptical about the virtues of meritocracy. A high level of mobility is likely to be socially destructive.
>
> Anthony Giddens

Allowing a person's circumstances to be determined partly by their abilities is a form of *elitism*, and hence viewed dimly in a mediocracy. The ultimate aim is to generate a world in which it will be regarded as unfair that someone should benefit in any way from their ability, whether innate or acquired.

Meanwhile, one can *pretend* to care about the system failing to be meritocratic enough. Selection in schools is opposed on the grounds that the non-selected are not given adequate scope. Whether people really care about anyone having scope (except perhaps their own children) is questionable, and the non-selection approach does not improve scope for anyone. However, it does legitimise hostility towards those who are good at exams.

Music

 Art form which expresses personal emotions and attempts to transcend the rational.

 Art form which represents the political conditions of its time and the prejudices associated with a composer's class.

> Rather than protecting music as a sublimely meaningless activity that has managed to escape social signification, I insist on treating it as a medium that participates in social formation. It is too important a cultural force to be shrouded by notions of Romantic transcendence.
>
> Professor Susan McClary, UCLA

No art form is allowed to escape the requirements of the mediocratic ethos. Music may seem relatively harmless, as it is hard to see how it could be making appropriate statements about the social condition, but that makes it in some ways all the more threatening. There must not be any area of life immune from the social searchlight. If something exists, it is social by definition, and hence we need to consider its compatibility with agreed ideological standards.

With musical drama, the decree that culture should express social reality becomes relatively easy to implement. Mediocratic opera productions emphasise the supposed political and sexual aspects of a piece, regardless of whether they were in the mind of the author.

Narrative

 Type of content considered necessary for literature, drama or discussion.

 Superfluous and elitist element which puts unnecessary strain on an audience.

> If postmodernism means suspicion towards meta-narratives then, given the most powerful narrative of the last 200 years has been that which told the tale of the West's destiny, Muslims should understand post-modernism as the de-centering of the West.
>
> Dr. S. Sayyid, Association of Muslim Social Scientists

Mediocracy does not hold with narrative. Narrative makes things too clear. It presents a version of reality, which implies it may be *true* or *false*. It requires analytical participation on the part of the audience rather than just emotional involvement.

Supposedly, we are to be cynical about narrative because it structures events in ways that involve assumptions or stereotypes. The implicit claim is that mediocracy is more realistic. The true threat of narrative, however, is that it is about reality rather than society. Depriving the audience of narrative engenders not realism, but loss of interest in reality.

The purpose of narrative-less culture is not to encourage us to question our assumptions, but to leave us confused and frustrated. The subliminal message is: accept you are too confined by limitations to comprehend the complexities of life. Give up trying to understand things, and let someone else – experts, or the government – do it for you.

New Economy

 Term for a society in which most people have a mobile phone and a personal computer.

 Radically new world in which none of the old rules apply.

We have gone from a vertical chain of command for value creation to a much more horizontal chain of command. How you manage horizontally requires a totally different set of skills.

Carly Fiorina, Hewlett Packard CEO

Instead of judging people by their ability to memorise, to think sequentially and to write good prose, we might measure intelligence by the ability to pinball around through knowledge and make imaginative patterns on the web.

James Burke, The Pinball Effect

The past must be continually rejected in a mediocracy. Not just because its non-mediocratic aspects need to be avoided, but because we cannot be allowed to suspect that what we used to have might be preferable. The slogans of mediocracy therefore exhort us not to be nostalgic: "things change", "the debate has moved on", "one cannot go backwards", and so on.

A useful device is the theory that the environment has been transformed out of all recognition by technology. Mediocracy, on this reading, is simply the response to an extraordinary new world in which all the rules have changed.

Objectivity

 The analysis of reality without personal bias.

 Spurious concept which posits the existence of a reality independent of social construction.

'Truth' is to be understood as a system of ordered procedures for the production, regulation, distribution, circulation and operation of statements.

Michel Foucault

There is no possibility of a wholly disinterested statement.

Terry Eagleton

In a mediocracy it is not considered possible for an individual to make a statement untainted by personal or ideological bias. It is regarded as a truism that perceptions and judgments depend on the observer's position in *social space*. This rejection of objectivity is designed to make it impossible for anyone to criticise the prevailing viewpoint.

Some mediocrats may worry that relativism potentially undermines the legitimacy of *reform* to make things even more mediocratic, in that it appears to assign equal validity to anti-mediocratic viewpoints. However, this fear is unnecessary, since the destruction of bourgeois culture turns out not to require validation by bourgeois standards of logic or consistency.

Obscenity

 Contravention of bourgeois sensitivities regarding sex, aggression or suffering.

 Contravention of egalitarian values.

> Vast wealth is generated in Britain, but look how it's divided – obscene wealth for a few, sitting alongside desperate poverty for too many.
>
> TUC General Secretary

There is nothing that mediocracy really finds obscene. It prides itself on its unshockability. Torture, unusual types of sex, bodily fluids, decapitation, painful death – such things are deemed acceptable material for representations, and one is expected to be able to stomach them.

Mediocracy likes to pretend, however, to be shocked and offended by inequality. This is not simply because it wants to make society more **equal**, but because it wants the *absence* of state intervention to be regarded as morally unacceptable.

Oppression

 Practices used to make life unpleasant for those who fall foul of prevailing ideology.

 Relation of the overprivileged to the underprivileged; anything which makes the latter feel bad.

North Wales Police is investigating a complaint made against Tony Blair over allegedly saying "f***ing Welsh" six years ago. Earlier this month, it was revealed that police spent nearly £4,000 investigating comments about Welsh people made by television presenter Anne Robinson on a BBC chat show.

BBC News

The real targets of oppression in a mediocracy are the middle class – academics, writers, managers, businessmen. These are the people who are to be harried and whose lives are to be ruined.

In any society, oppression requires a rationalisation. In mediocracy, the excuse is that the person persecuted is himself being 'oppressive' towards the *underprivileged* – by speaking or behaving in a way which might offend them, or which might conceivably lead to bad behaviour towards them by others.

Those who decide whether someone is guilty of this are not the supposed victims. They are members of the middle class themselves – politicians, journalists, university administrators.

Parent

 The person most likely to promote the interests of a child.

 Surrogate carer acting in lieu of state agent, at risk of abusing and subject to monitoring.

If parenting is so important, we cannot abandon it to the vagaries of the individual.

Margaret Hodge, Minister for Children

Margaret Hodge, former leader of Islington council, tried to block a programme on abuse in Islington children's homes. She wrote to the BBC to condemn the programme and called Demetrious Panton, who spoke to the BBC, "extremely disturbed". Mr. Panton, now a government consultant, said Islington council had repeatedly ignored claims he had been abused as a child by the head of his children's home.

Guardian

A mediocracy does not approve of private childcare, because there is a risk that a parent will not transmit mediocratic values, and may even try to give a child *advantages*. The mediocratic parent's responsibilities are therefore limited to providing board and lodging.

Intervention is rationalised in terms of 'best interests of the child'. However, there is no real concern with protecting any one child, let alone doing it good; only a desire to promote **equality** by ensuring all children are under the control of the state.

Philosophy

 Investigating the ultimate nature of existence.

✓ **The use of abstruse verbiage to demonstrate that philosophical 'problems' are spurious.**

L' is language L augmented with the truth predicate 'true-in-L', which is 'mental'. In L (and hence L') it is possible to pick out, with a definite description, each sentence in the extension of the truth predicate, but if L is consistent there exists no predicate of syntax (of the 'physical' vocabulary), no matter how complex, that applies to all and only the true sentences of L. There can be no 'psychophysical law' in the form of a biconditional '(x) (x is true-in-L if and only if x is ∂)' where '∂' is replaced by a 'physical' predicate (a predicate of L).

Professor Donald Davidson on the mind-body relationship

Old-fashioned philosophers analysed the assumptions of conventional thinking. In doing so, they often questioned prevailing ideological assumptions to a degree that made others in their societies uncomfortable.

Not surprisingly, mediocracy seeks to neutralise or eliminate philosophy. As with other disciplines, this is best achieved from the inside. Philosophy must be made so boring that it repels anyone tempted to engage in it for more traditional reasons, such as wanting to understand reality. It must be made to appeal only to those who enjoy ***technicality*** for its own sake.

Philosopher

 Person who tries to advance understanding of the fundamental nature of reality.

 Person employed to do *philosophy*.

 Intellectual who supports egalitarianism by means of *boggling* and *blurring*.

I will begin with the question 'where?'. Not directly with the question 'where are we?' or 'where have we come to?' but 'where does the question of the right to philosophy take place?', which can be immediately translated by 'where ought it take place?' Where does it find today its most appropriate place? The very form of this question concerning a question – namely 'where? in what place can a question take place?' – supposes that between the question and the place, between the question of the question and the question of the place, there be a sort of implicit contract, a supposed affinity, as if a question should always be first authorized by a place, legitimated in advance by a determined space that makes it both rightful and meaningful, thus making it possible and by the same token necessary, both legitimate and inevitable. According to the French idiom – and already the usage of this idiom, the effective authority of this idiom, brings us back to the question of the cosmopolitical [... etc.]

Jacques Derrida speaking to UNESCO

A post-philosophical culture would contain nobody called 'Philosopher' who could explain why certain areas of culture enjoyed a special relation to reality.

Professor Richard Rorty

To the extent that mediocrats permit an activity called 'philosophy' to take place, such activity must support mediocratic ideology by means of appropriate pseudo-analysis. This may be necessary in the transition to full mediocracy.

Ultimately, however, any activity with a family resemblance to original philosophy is too dangerous. Even with the *technicality* requirement imposed, there is too great a risk that some real analysis might slip through the net. Real analysis can never be helpful, given that mediocracy is predicated on deception.

This is why we see a desire for capitulation in mediocratic philosophy. Mediocratic philosophers compete in their eagerness to announce that the enterprise is hopeless, and that the quest for philosophical knowledge is doomed to failure.

Physicalism

Sarah Kane's play *Cleansed* concerns the inhabitants of an institution under the control of a torturer/psychiatrist named Tinker. Limbs are removed, skins removed, genitals removed, and identities forcibly changed. *Cleansed* is a punishing experience, yet it seems surprisingly redemptive.

Royal Court Theatre education pack

If mediocrity can be said to be characterised by anything as definite as a belief, then two beliefs are key: *egalitarianism*, the belief that people are all the same, and *physicalism*, the belief that everything is material.

Physicalism implies that individuals are driven by mechanical forces, that they are manipulable and predictable, and that they do not possess free will or even a meaningful self.

Physiology

 Something whose direct representation outside medicine is considered offensive.

 An important part of *realism*, **hence promoted through representations in art, television, etc.**

The *Body Worlds* exhibition shows a dead chess player at his board, his skull sliced open to reveal his brain. A skinless corpse sits astride a horse, clutching two brains – his and the horse's. A woman is shown with her stomach opened to reveal a foetus. Professor Gunther von Hagens insists his work is aesthetic and educational.

Daily Telegraph

Physiology combines two of mediocracy's favourite themes: the body (supportive of *equality*, i.e. homogeneity), and *realism* (i.e. the desire to disgust).

Mediocracy takes pleasure in forcibly confronting us with the objects of our own distaste. We must not be allowed to escape awareness that what is *inside* us is not something interesting, complex and psychological, but the sticky messiness of entrails.

Politicise

 To interpret something in the light of leftist ideology.

 To place something in its correct social and historical context.

> I was telling my mother about a conversation with David Mamet in which I asked whether he thought his play *Oleanna* was more about academia than sexual politics. She said, "That is ridiculous – academia is about sexual politics. You cannot separate them."
>
> Julia Stiles, actress

In mediocracy, culture becomes a social activity rather than the product of individuals. It is to be considered as a *given* that everything is political, and that it is bourgeois to regard art or science as exceptions.

Taking a position on issues such as wealth redistribution, or affirmative action, is an essential component of being a mediocratic cultural producer. Campaigning for 'change' (i.e. the elimination of remaining pockets of non-mediocracy) becomes the ethical norm rather than the exception.

In most mediocratic cultural fields, the term *politicise* is therefore redundant. In literature, for example, it is standard to view texts politically; to do otherwise would be considered bizarre.

Pop star

 Entertainer who panders to adolescent fantasies.

 Rich celebrity who promotes egalitarianism.

I represent a lot of people who have no voice at all.

Bono

I think shareholders are the greatest evil of this modern world. Deadlines mean nothing to us. We'll sink our record company if we have to.

Chris Martin, lead singer of Coldplay

While mediocracy frowns on the idea of heroes, the mass must be permitted a certain amount of celebrity worship for therapeutic purposes. There should therefore be high profile spokesmen for mediocratic ideology drawn from outside the government. These should be popular entertainers or sportsmen rather than producers of high culture, as their message is more likely to reach a wide audience.

Mediocracy will grant economic advantages to such persons in exchange for promulgating socially correct values, meaning such things as *assertiveness*, egalitarianism and *cartoonisation*.

Poverty

 State of being very poor.

Condition of an individual whose income is less than half the national average, or who lacks one or more of the following: television, freezer, mobile phone, tumble drier, car.

> A lot of theory about capitalism forgets that there are soup kitchens in America, and that a quarter of pre-school children live in poverty.
>
> Professor Ted Honderich

One of the main justifications for the political programmes of mediocracy is a supposed concern for the *underprivileged*. It follows that, to sustain mediocracy, it must always be possible to identify a class of people whose conditions are regarded as unacceptable and who therefore call for additional intervention.

This can be achieved in two ways. First, by ensuring that the conditions regarded as unacceptable never actually improve. Second, by continually changing the definitions of what constitutes 'unacceptable'.

A type of poverty *not* highlighted in a mediocracy is that which arises from having to rely on state services that are run on mediocratic principles and hence do not function properly – e.g. medicine, education, policing.

Principle

 Something adhered to because it reflects an important value.

 Undesirable obstacle to what the community's representatives think best.

> In a meeting, Tony Blair banged the table, demanding to know "why the f***" it was impossible to rewrite human rights laws to allow action against a terrorist threat. He kept asking "Why can't we do this?". Three weeks later he got his way, sweeping aside the caveats of his officials.
>
> *Observer*

Mediocracy dislikes principles, with the possible exception of *equality*, i.e. that people should be regarded as identical. A principle is too much like a statement about objective reality. The idea that something might be important independently of current fashionable thinking – for example, sanctity of life, or lawyer-client confidentiality – conflicts with the consensus model of reality. A principle implies something which might need to be fought for, and this is inconsistent with mediocratic *indifference*.

People *may* of course find it easier to stick to something (e.g. punctuality) if they believe in it as a principle than if they are pointed towards its utilitarian benefits – 'makes life better for others', 'helps to avoid train crashes', etc. However, to criticise mediocracy for weaknesses in its anti-principle approach is to miss the point. Mediocracy is not trying to maintain the same benefits without the principles. Mediocracy is primarily concerned with only one thing: the assertion of mediocracy.

Progress

 Improvements in technology which reduce the need for state activity.

 The replacement of bourgeois culture with egalitarian culture.

The excellence of our universities depends on drawing upon the widest pool of talent – making change inevitable and necessary.

Gordon Brown

The cultural aspect of the new state will, above all, be negative, directed towards criticism of the past, obliterating it from memory and destroying it.

Antonio Gramsci

Mediocracy prides itself on being *progressive*. Its critics (to the extent they are permitted to survive, and allowed to express themselves) are derided as conservative, reactionary, and so on. However, the kind of progress that mediocracy promotes is rather specific. Curiously, it often takes tribal life as its paradigm. Movement 'forwards' is movement towards a model of a pacifist, egalitarian community, not exploiting its environment, sharing all tasks equally, with each member answerable to the whole community.

Other kinds of change are considered inappropriate, and therefore not described as 'progressive': e.g. greater freedom from state interference, fewer restrictions on commercial activity.

Public service

 Service which individuals want but markets do not provide.

 Service which exists to reinforce communitarian values.

Why do we believe so passionately in public services? Because they are what community is all about. They bind us together. ... Public services will never be just another customer service.

Tony Blair

The goods of the public domain must not be treated as commodities. Performance indicators are out of place. People are not consumers in the public domain, they are citizens. Professionals must have the autonomy to exercise judgement as they see fit.

Professor David Marquand

In a mediocracy it is not considered crucial to the success of a public service whether it actually works. The more important objective is to generate social cohesion. A public service is therefore an ideal sink for absorbing excess national product, in order to avoid generating undesirable individual liberty.

Mediocracy likes to promote the argument that certain areas (e.g. medicine, education) must be administered publicly, because of supposed market imperfections, or because individuals do not conform to mediocratic notions of rationality. The idea that the decisions of state agents may be *less* rational, rather than more, is carefully avoided.

Publicity

 Observation by the mass, to which a person may choose to expose himself.

 The right of the mass to inspect an individual.

Reality TV means the further democratisation of showbiz. What sad, resentful, hierarchy-respecting, forelock-tugging bit of us is so upset by this harmless, righteous, glitter-dusted revolution?

Julie Burchill

In a mediocracy, power is with society. And society wants everyone to be answerable to it, or at least observable. Privacy is not considcred a right. It may be permitted if society happens not to be interested. However, with advances in technology the number of areas which society cannot be bothered to scrutinise is shrinking.

The nature of the searchlight depends on whether it is the mass, or agents of the elite, who are doing the observing. When the *mass* calls the individual to account, the issue is one of social acceptability. Do we like this person? What have they done for us lately? Are they attractive? Are they useful? Do they conform to social norms? If not, are they at least funny? Are they prepared to degrade themselves for our amusement?

Television programmes in which we observe people's unrehearsed behaviour are often dismissed as little more than cheap entertainment. But in fact they are important assertions of mass power, and of the implied right of mediocracy to inspect every aspect of an individual's life.

Quality

 High standard of output or content.

 Level of training.

 Compliance with contemporary norms.

> After Duchamp's *Fountain*, the meaning of the term
> 'art' is irreversibly changed. Non-art invades art, and
> the meaning of art has become undecidable. Art is no
> longer a pure concept to which we can appeal in order
> to judge Tracey Emin's *Bed*.
>
> Belsey, *Poststructuralism*

Modern philosophers have argued that whether something is judged as true/real/good in a society depends on whether those in power give their imprimatur to the judgement. Mediocracy expands this argument by asserting that, since there are no standards other than the social one, what is true/real/good *just is* whatever society says is true/real/good.

In a mediocracy the definition of *good* culture – in spite of much **boggling** over the issue – is therefore straightforward: it is whatever official practitioners say it is. Good philosophy is simply what authorised philosophers do; good art is what authorised artists do. There can be no alternative criterion.

Quantity

 Crude and simplistic measure of achievement.

 Primary criterion by which to judge success.

> In terms of quantities at least, the contemporary
> visual arts have literally never been so successful.
>
> Paul Greenhalgh, President, Nova Scotia College of Arts

> Accident & Emergency patients nearing the end of
> the four-hour wait designated as a maximum by the
> government are routinely moved out of A&E and into
> holding areas, so that they can be classified as having
> been dealt with. Sometimes these areas are little more
> than rooms next to A&E units, or even corridors.
>
> *Daily Telegraph*

With everyone *equal* (i.e. identical), the principal measure of
merit or success in a mediocracy is number of people. If more
students are passing examinations, more books are being read, and
more theatre tickets are being sold, culture must be doing well.

A predilection for counting turns into a more general obsession with
measurement. The benefits of measurement are that it:

- avoids the need for thinking,
- can be used to skate over underlying problems,
- conveys the idea of society *assessing* individuals, and
- reinforces egalitarianism by assuming uniformity in the units
  being counted.

Radical

 Implying a break with prevailing intellectual or moral conventions.

 Term for culture which criticises bourgeois concepts such as individuality or privacy.

> The concept of culture grew up as a critique of middle-class society, not as an ally of it.
>
> Terry Eagleton

Mediocracy, like *1984*'s Oceania, requires its audience to believe in a continual need for ideological battle. Although the war has been won, and everyone has absorbed the required beliefs, the fight against the former enemy (capitalism, Christianity, conservatism, etc.) can never cease. Any sign of resistance must be treated as proof that the enemies of mediocracy are still powerful.

Under mediocracy, the 'discoveries' of modernism – *reflexivity*, secularism, loss of the self, social construction, etc. – have been fully assimilated. Yet mediocratic culture continues to assault the straw man of traditionalism, who can somehow never be quite dead enough.

It is important that critique of the non-mediocratic continues to carry the 'radical' label, however much such critique has become dogma.

Realism

 Awareness of reality (= everything which exists).

 Emphasis on 'reality' (= the primitive, the brutal, the degrading).

 The belief that there is no room for bourgeois escapism.

> This is not a movie you'd recommend to a friend unless he's into torture and sadism. A death scene lasts for an excruciating six minutes. The film disgusted and made me feel physically sick in parts. The mother's screams are harrowing and human, and you really forget you are watching a film. 9 out of 10.
>
> Review of Michael Haneke's *Funny Games*

The mediocratic audience is forcibly presented with the things that make it uncomfortable: physiology, suffering, the sleazier aspects of sex, disability, violence, war, starvation, etc. Mediocratic wildlife documentaries, for example, are shot in the style of sexy horror movies, with the rationale that the killing of animals should be shown in its full glory as a true representation of nature.

In effect, *realism* is a form of aggression against those members of the audience who find its presentations offensive. However, the aggression is *legitimised* by reference to the fact that the sensibilities being offended can be regarded as bourgeois. The point is not to make people more aware of reality, but to make them feel hopeless and degraded. A dejected person is more likely to surrender to the collective, and is therefore more useful to mediocracy.

Reflexivity

 Undermining one's own field in order to make it repellent to other potential participants.

 Application of *awareness* to a field in order to rescue it from bourgeois assumptions.

> Self-reflexive, postmodernist concern with language and form highlighted the wider powers of commercial and political interests. Authors who drew most attention to their own form and language were in this way among the most politically committed.
>
> *Oxford English Literary History*

Fake self-analysis is another weapon in the armoury of mediocratic pseudo-intellectualism, along with **challenge, radicalism**, and so on. It looks clever to seem to be examining the foundations of your own discipline, until one realises that the results of the examination are predetermined. Like other mediocratic analyses, the conclusions must always be consistent with the prevailing ideology.

Pseudo-reflexivity has a number of objectives, but genuine analysis is not among them. The mediocratic dissection of literature/philosophy/etc. serves to undermine all attempts at real literature/philosophy/etc. It soon becomes impossible to say anything in any subject without an element of mockery, or without the anxious examination of the subject's supposed foundations.

Rehabilitation

 Rewriting history.

 Reassessing historical figures in order to show them as consistent with egalitarian values.

> Newton was an obsessive with a secret Swiss boyfriend. And, in the world of BBC4's *The Mark Steel Lectures*, he likes Alphabetti Spaghetti and the Communards. The contradictions of this fascinating character, half-scientist, half-magician, take us from his childhood penchant for arson to the Houses of Parliament via Old Compton Street.
>
> Open University online

In a mediocracy, we must not be reminded that there used to be a world in which some individuals were not mere ciphers. Historical figures therefore have to be portrayed in a 'proletarian' style, in order to show them as people who would be compatible with mediocratic values and acceptable to a mass audience – in other words, like characters in a blue collar soap.

Ideally, references to exceptional historical figures (geniuses, military heroes, etc.) should be eliminated, since they encourage the idea that individuals can be significant. On the other hand, as the Soviet revolutionaries found, it may be simpler to remould rather than abolish existing bourgeois culture, since building a replacement culture from scratch can be tiring. A more convenient strategy is therefore to subtly deprecate such figures, or alternatively to show that they were in greater sympathy with egalitarian values than had been realised.

Research

 Work done to find things out about reality.

 Technically proficient output of *academics*.

The question is not *should* science be controlled,
but *how* can science be controlled most effectively?
Allocating resources must be done in the context of
politically directed goals set by the community.

Professors Hilary Rose and Steven Rose

Academic research in a mediocracy is produced in enormous
quantities, but most of it is not intended for consumption. Its
purpose is to crowd out genuine intellectual activity, while concealing
the resulting deficit by means of imposing bulk. A secondary function
is to police the academic profession by forcing members to churn
out vacuous but technically sophisticated verbiage at a high rate, to
ensure that only those who are comfortable with pointlessness are
permitted to practise.

Empirical research must appear to be assiduously painstaking, and
should use abstruse statistics. *Theoretical* research must comply
with the rules of **academic theory**. *Scientific* research should
involve theories or technologies which reinforce **physicalism** and/
or egalitarianism. Research in *non-scientific* areas should promote
egalitarian ideology, or provide perspectives for criticising bourgeois
concepts. The meaningful content of research papers should be
minimal, but expressed using complex terminology as proof of the
writer's credentials.

Responsibility

 A person's sense that he is in charge of areas relating to property or personal relationships.

 A person's moral liability for wrongs carried out by other members of his class or race.

> If your conception of the person includes the unconscious positions you occupy, responsibility can be expanded. This calls you to responsibility for events and structures – of racism and sexism for instance – that you did not explicitly intend.
>
> Professor Jonathan Culler

Mediocratic *responsibility* is a concept designed to make the individual feel humble via-à-vis his new god, Society. Mediocracy wants everyone, especially the bourgeoisie, to be on the defensive. We are to feel permanently mortified about the harm we are told was done in the past to women, to the working class, and to various indigenous peoples.

No amount of compensating or genuflecting can ever expiate our guilt as members of supposedly repressive social groups. The point is not, however, to rectify genuine grievances, or to prevent future ones. The point is to generate a certain atmosphere in which bourgeois intellectuals are automatically suspect and hence too busy feeling guilty to criticise the prevailing ideology.

A variant on the responsibility theme is the idea that we are *complicit* in anything which occurs in our society. The point here is that, however objectionable the manifestations of mediocracy, one cannot complain because one is somehow involved in causing them.

Right

 An individual's legitimised claim for freedom from interference.

 The legitimised claim of society to interfere with an individual.

 An individual's claim for state support.

Amnesty International plans more campaigning for rights to food and water, and less focus on individual cases. "We at Amnesty have been part of creating this little magic territory of human rights that's just civil and political. But before people get to political rights they want to know what to do about Aids and food."

Financial Times

The founders of the Soviet state created a constitution with a plethora of rights which they simply couldn't afford to grant, rightly supposing that nobody would be reckless enough to insist on them being observed.

Vladimir Bukovsky

Mediocratic rights function as a propaganda device. They are not there to grant anyone real, unconditional claims, but to displace pre-mediocratic rights, i.e. civil liberties. Once enough new rights have been granted to swamp earlier ones, the term can be devalued so that an individual's 'right' means 'something which *may* be taken into account along with the state's and everyone else's claims'. (A similar approach is applied to *liberties*.)

Ruling class

 Liberal **elite who dominate politics and culture.**

 Wealthy people who secretly wield their power to influence government and the economy.

> You cannot force people to obey by violence, as the Soviet system tried to do. So you need systems of indoctrination to ensure that they agree to what the ruling groups want to do.
>
> Professor Noam Chomsky

> Today, thanks to Noam Chomsky, it is almost axiomatic that public opinion in 'free market' democracies is manufactured just like sliced bread.
>
> Arundhati Roy

Like a communist regime's never-ending war against the enemies of the proletariat, mediocracy needs to retain a dummy concept of 'ruling class' to act as the target for resentment, and to deflect criticism from the real puppetmasters.

Thus the *ruling class* in a mediocracy is not the cultural elite, or the bureaucrats and state agents with power over every area of life, it is the aristocracy, corporations or wealthy shareholders.

It is a mediocratic truism that the harder it is to detect the machinations of this mythical ruling class, the more successfully they are concealing themselves, and hence the more forcefully they need to be exposed and penalised.

Sacking

 Ousting someone from their job because they are bad at it.

 Ousting someone from their job because they have expressed an unacceptable viewpoint.

You and I have been given two hands and two legs. Some people have not been born like that for a reason. The karma is working from another lifetime.

Glenn Hoddle, 30 January 1999

Glenn Hoddle has been sacked as England's soccer coach after it became clear he had lost the confidence of football fans, the public and that of Tony Blair.

Daily Telegraph, 3 February 1999

An enormous number of academics were expelled and censured to make the university amenable to the regimentation of scholarship.

Bracher, *The German Dictatorship*

Representatives of mediocratic institutions are expected to act in sympathy with the objectives and philosophies agreed by the community's representatives, i.e. the elite.

If they deviate from this, or criticise the prevailing ideology, or criticise colleagues for conforming to the ideology, they are to be dismissed.

Safety

 Something individuals arrange for themselves by taking care.

 Something the state must arrange by criminalising all possible sources of risk.

> The College believes that more regulation is required if we are to control the advertising excesses of the food industry. The College supports fully the Children's Food Bill and its commitment towards better food and a healthier future.
>
> Royal College of Physicians of Edinburgh

A mediocracy does not actually *care* whether people are protected from risks. Particularly not certain types of risk, such as the risk of being killed by slapdash state medicine, or the risk of being psychologically damaged by state schools. But the concept of **safety** is a good way to legitimise interfering in people's lives, in their supposed interests. It is therefore invoked at every opportunity.

An obsession with safety may appear to indicate a culture of overprotection. In reality, it is about policing everyone's lives, and making them aware that nothing they do is exempt from public scrutiny, or from the need to obtain permission from society.

As with other mediocratic phenomena that cause unease, it is desirable to blame capitalism whenever possible. Criticisms should refer to 'compensation culture', and to the excesses of the legal market, rather than to the concept of an interventionist state.

Scholar

 Person engaged in the pursuit of knowledge for its own sake.

 Person who aims to provide intellectual support for egalitarianism.

The concept of the university as a community of scholars can be only a very limited justification for the state to fund universities. It is the wider social and economic role of universities that justifies state financial support.

Charles Clarke, Education Minister

Research and learning were assigned their new functions in the Nazi regime: scholarship as an end in itself would have to give way to the goal of 'völkische Weltanschauung' and unity.

Bracher, *The German Dictatorship*

In mediocracy, passion for an intellectual subject (e.g. philosophy, classics, literature) is considered incompatible with the correct level of *awareness*. It is too solitary, and may lead to unsuitable feelings of intensity. It also tends to be associated with other concepts that are considered dubious, such as objectivity, reality and knowledge.

The purpose of *mediocratic* study is to reinforce bonds with the community, either by way of communal activities with other *academics*, or by generating intellectual reinforcement for egalitarianism.

School

 Place for learning facts and skills.

 Place for institutionalised socialisation.

In a community academy, a pupil might arrive for breakfast, have a health check in the afternoon, and stay on for an after school club. Students learn about society and community. The school's sponsor Andrew Rosenfeld said: "The aim is to put community responsibility at the forefront of the curriculum, and to instil the idea that a commitment to others is every bit as important as academic and financial success."

Guardian

In a mediocracy, people who attend state schools are psychologically handicapped for life. Fortunately for the status quo, those with a handicap would rather not admit it, while those who manage to avoid the state system are happy to keep quiet about their advantages.

Without the financial incentive of keeping parents satisfied, the motivations of those involved in education become unclear. Do they wish to give their pupils an advantage over other pupils? Surely not, given the inconsistency of this with wider social interests.

Science

 Objective knowledge acquired in a spirit of dispassionate enquiry.

 The quest for theories and data supportive of *physicalism* **and** *egalitarianism*.

> The old excuse that scientists are not to blame for the crimes committed by demagogues won't wash. Scientists have had a direct responsibility for acts for which we should now feel collectively ashamed.
>
> *New Scientist* editorial

Mediocracy rests on the premise that there are no significant innate differences between individuals. Providing this thesis with support is a key objective for the mediocratic intelligentsia. Persuading people of the mediocratic perspective is achieved by relentlessly stressing those characteristics which a person has in common with everyone else, while forcefully undermining ideas about individual differences.

There is great enthusiasm among mediocratic academics for the idea that everything human is explicable by reference to biology and chemistry. The predictive successes of the physical sciences may explain part of the attraction, but the fanaticism exhibited in certain cases suggests the presence of ideological motives.

Security

 What governments do to protect citizens from criminal or military attack.

 Generic term for arguments that show the case for liberty to be hopelessly weak.

The home secretary Charles Clarke says he will lock away for five years anyone who "glorifies, exalts or celebrates" a terrorist act committed in the past 20 years. If someone, somewhere takes anything you say or write as encouraging to terror, even if they do not act on it, you have committed a criminal act.

Guardian

The possibility of invoking emergency powers offered a convenient escape from political responsibility, and prepared the population for the type of authoritarian ideas which were being bandied about with growing force by propagandists and in the universities.

Bracher, *The German Dictatorship*

D oes mediocratic government loathe and fear the threat of war, of terror, or of rioting? No, it welcomes such threats.

A ***crisis*** – real, imagined or manufactured – is one of the best ways to legitimise the mediocratic agenda: to oppress and persecute the individual, preferably with the excuse that it is for the good of the community.

Self

 Unitary identity associated with an individual.

 Illusory concept arising from misuse of language, proven by *research* to be fictitious.

> It is often suggested that our illusory sense of selfhood is a product of cultural conditioning, but this is a way of dodging the issue. The findings of cognitive science show that we are hard-wired for the illusion of self.
>
> Professor John Gray

Mediocracy does not like the notion of *self*, any more than it likes the notions of *individual* or *consciousness*. The group is everything, the individual a bourgeois category mistake.

By means of mediocratic pseudoanalysis, the concept of self can be made to disappear. All we need is a bit of **boggling**, a few references to the difficulty of **meaning**, some post-Kantian doubts about the external world, and we can prove what we like – in this case, that the self does not exist.

Such philosophical analysis needs to be used selectively, so that only appropriate conclusions are reached. This is why it is essential to receive approved academic training before being permitted to pronounce on philosophical issues.

Service

 Doing what a customer wants.

Interacting with customers in ways that promote the values of the service provider.

> Educating more people to university level shrinks the pool of people able to do lower-skilled work. This helps to stabilise their wages, because there are fewer people available to do those jobs. It is no accident that plumbers can charge $75 an hour or that good housekeepers or cooks are hard to find.
>
> Thomas Friedman, *The World is Flat*

The word 'service' comes from the verb 'to serve', which originally meant to act in accordance with another person's wishes. In mediocracy, however, the idea of one individual simply doing what another individual wants is too threatening.

'Service' therefore has to be redefined, shifting emphasis from individual to social preferences, and from wishes to *interests*. There may be references to 'customers', 'choice' and so on, but these are superficial. They prove necessary because without them, service providers are liable to be too preoccupied with corporate culture to remember customers at all.

The concept of ***individualism*** proves useful in this context. People are taught to find it demeaning to serve (in the original sense), encouraged to believe that they should not have to do so, and to feel, instead, that they have a right to exercise their judgement and creativity.

Service professional

 Person employed to provide services.

✓ **Person employed to supervise or assess persons who provide *services*.**

This week we held a reception for front-line staff, many of whose jobs didn't even exist before. New Deal advisers, Sure Start workers, nurse consultants, Community Support Officers, NHS Direct staff, classroom assistants. All giving us the capacity to help thousands upon thousands in new ways.

Tony Blair

Why did people become Stasi informers? "Well, some were convinced of the cause. But I think it was mainly because informers got the feeling that they were somebody. They felt they had it over other people."

Anna Funder, Stasiland

A mediocratic service professional is a person employed within a service sector, occasionally to provide the service itself, but more typically in an ancillary capacity, e.g. target inspector, training adviser, gender relations counsellor, equal access watchdog.

The number of service professionals employed in a given sector is regarded as an index of the **quality** of service provided.

Sex

 Bonding activity between individuals in a highly developed relationship.

 Social activity performed for purposes of psychological hygiene.

> Measured by the neutral scale of theory rather than simply accepting the results of western history, it seems relatively obvious that sex is political.
>
> Professor Linda Hirshman, Brandeis

In mediocracy, the concept of sex is crucial. It is seen as the main driving force of the individual, and the key cultural ingredient. Its ideological function is to prove we are all equal, i.e. equally mechanical. It is emphasised in every area of cultural output, from advertising to opera, sociology to literary criticism. It is portrayed as being, at the same time, both supremely important and irredeemably trivial.

Sex is the criterion of normality in a mediocracy. Abstinence is unhealthy, low levels of sexual activity a sign of psychopathology calling for treatment. Successful sex requires training, which is to be provided from an early age by the education system.

The point is not to encourage toleration of human desires, but to celebrate our degradation. This is achieved by means of an ambivalent attitude, promoting sex on the one hand while sneering at it on the other. Sex is to be regarded as invalidating any idealistic or romantic notions that people might have, particularly about themselves.

Sex is presented as individualistic, but is used to emphasise our role as social agents entering into adult community activities. An individual's sexuality and sexual activity become matters with a public dimension. They are available for inspection by society, with mass media playing an important role in providing *publicity*.

In a mediocracy, a person's allegiance to their sexual partner is at odds with their allegiance to society. The partnership over, any loyalty to the other person evaporates, and they may decide to pass information about them to the community, or to punish them for socially unacceptable behaviour on behalf of the collective.

A mediocracy inundates its citizens with advice on mechanical procedures, e.g. how to use contraceptives. One is expected to be proficient at the physical aspects of sex, which are assumed to be the same for everyone. Psychological aspects are considered relatively unimportant. This is consistent with the model of the individual as a predictable entity with no meaningful inner life.

Society

 Shorthand term for a large group of individuals.

 Ultimate origin of all significance.

There *is* such a thing as society. We are not isolated individuals but achieve our best fulfilment in the relationship between individual and community.

Chris Smith, Minister for Culture

Society is the complete unity of man with nature.

Marx

Mediocracy seeks to eliminate the undesirable side effect of capitalism, i.e. freedom from control by the collective. However, this has to be done subtly. The issue of society versus the individual is a sensitive one, and stating one's position too clearly may evoke resistance. It is better to imply, rather than assert, that the individual is subordinated to society. The best way to do this is subliminally, using cultural output.

It is easy to make emphasis on the social appear virtuous. Being more 'social' surely means being more willing to help other people? But with mediocracy that is not the point. There is plenty of state *welfare* financed by involuntary subscription, and much head-scratching about the problems of people in remote places. However, helpfulness towards people in one's immediate vicinity (neighbours, relatives, casualties on the street) is considered unnecessary and no longer practised.

Student

 Person of high intelligence studying an academic subject to an advanced level.

 Person taking up a state-sponsored training course in socio-cultural studies.

> Stop saying to the children of those who have not gone to university in the past that there is a charmed circle of educational achievement and it has big 'keep out' signs all around it.
>
> David Miliband, Minister for School Standards

> Enrolment of students in 1920s Russia was subjected to class criteria to exclude 'bourgeois' applicants, i.e. children of the middle class.
>
> Kolakowski, *Main Currents of Marxism*

Mediocracy cannot tolerate the idea of a product being consumed only among a select group, especially when the principle of selection is intelligence. It is therefore regarded as unacceptable for some people not to go to university.

In order to make a university suitable for everyone, its activities must become *inclusive*. Entrance requirements must become less elitist, which can be achieved by modifying examinations so that they cease to be biased in favour of intellect, or by basing entry on the ability to demonstrate social skills, or simply by discriminating against intelligence.

Stupid

 Critical term indicating lack of sense.

Term of approval for culture that does not have any pretensions to stimulating thought.

What is 'Wal-Mart'? Is it, like, they sell wall stuff?

Paris Hilton, TV star

Mandelstam* always said they knew what they were doing: the aim was to destroy not only people, but the intellect itself.

Nadezhda Mandelstam

It is not that genuine stupidity is celebrated in a mediocracy, since nothing is really celebrated in a mediocracy except mediocracy. People of low intelligence are belittled for their particular deficiencies as readily as anyone else is for theirs. What is promoted, rather, is *identification* with stupidity.

Enthusiasm for 'stupidity' can express a rejection of the supposed 'intelligence' of mediocratic high culture, which in practice is dull and impenetrable. This suits the mediocratic elite, who create such culture precisely to turn everyone else off it.

The development of a celebrity class which is predominantly glamorous, rich and 'stupid' indicates what the real threat in a mediocracy is perceived to be. Not extreme financial inequality, not fame, not desirability, but intellect – the genuine rather than the ersatz kind.

---

* Osip Mandelstam, Russian poet who died in a Soviet labour camp.

Taboo

 Prohibition of a practice which is likely to offend bourgeois sensibilities.

 Prohibition of a hypothesis which conflicts with egalitarian values.

Every time BBC Radio 4's *Today* programme considers inviting journalist Nick Cohen on to debate some topic, a researcher calls him the previous night and 'tests' whether he is going to say the 'right' thing. If he is not, he isn't allowed on air.

New Statesman

If I write a play that is not daring, or shocking, or sensational, I am less likely to win funding for it.

Rachel Wagstaff

In a mediocracy certain kinds of proposition (e.g. 'ability is inherited') are so ideologically dangerous that they become inexpressible.

Research which might support such theories is prohibited. Data which appears to favour them is presumed to be flawed. Individuals who express anything other than total rejection of them are normally **sacked**.

Technicality

 Pointless formalism, used to conceal lack of meaning and to prevent criticism.

 The use of complex techniques in modern cultural output, indicating sophistication.

> There are texts of theory that resist meaning
> so powerfully that the very process of failing to
> comprehend the text is part of what it has to offer.
>
> *Critical Terms for Literary Study*

The key theme of mediocratic high culture is *vacuity*, i.e. the absence of meaningful content. Content is too threatening because it might conflict with mediocratic ideology, and is too reminiscent of the idea that reality might be objective rather than socially constructed.

In order to retain the appearance of robust cultural disciplines, mediocracy needs alternative proofs and justifications for their existence, and an alternative criterion for producer status. The alternative is provided by *technicality*.

Technicality, which includes the use of jargon and complex techniques, is vacuous but highly demanding. It therefore functions successfully as an intellectual absorbent, distracting both practitioners and audience from attending to the absence of meaningful content.

Fashion is crucial to technicality, as it is necessary to exclude practitioners with inappropriate motivation, e.g. those wishing to challenge mediocracy. Not any technicality will do therefore; it must be of the type currently approved by the relevant professional elite.

Terrorism

 Violence against capitalist states.

✓ **Violence that is incompatible with egalitarian values.**

> A majority of those killed in the 9/11 attack might be more accurately viewed as 'little Eichmanns' – i.e. a cadre of faceless bureaucrats and technical experts who willingly (and profitably) harnessed themselves to the task of making America's genocidal world order hum with maximum efficiency – than as 'innocents'.
>
> Professor Ward Churchill, University of Colorado

> The word 'terrorist' can be a barrier to understanding. We should try to avoid using the term.
>
> BBC guidelines to journalists

Terrorism represents hostility to bourgeois values, and should therefore be viewed sympathetically. It is likely that the actions of terrorists are based on justified *anger*. The appropriate response may be to welcome their operations as suitable chastisement for capitalist excesses.

A significant benefit of terrorism is that it legitimises the removal of civil liberties. A threat to national security, or a risk to the safety of civilians, provides an apparently irrefutable justification for removing restrictions on the oppression of individuals by agents of the state.

Theft

 Appropriating another person's property.

 Possessing more than the average person.

> All centrally governed, nonegalitarian societies
> function as kleptocracies, transferring net wealth from
> commoners to upper classes.
>
> Jared Diamond

Mediocracy likes concepts that undermine the claims of the bourgeois individual. The idea that property is theft is a long-favoured one, invoking the old model of 'everything belongs to the tribe'.

The argument that a bourgeois phenomenon which seems to be one thing is 'really' another, unacceptable thing, can be used either to cast aspersions on the bourgeois phenomenon, or to legitimise the other thing.*

Since inequality supposedly represents covert confiscation of other people's property, then if we permit inequality, we should have no objection to governments confiscating property through taxation or otherwise, and should be relatively tolerant of burglary.

---

* The reverse argument, in which an objectionable phenomenon is claimed
  to be equivalent to something which we already tolerate, can be equally
  valuable. Thus if we allow advertisements that set out to offend, supposedly
  in a good cause, we should not object to equally offensive art or theatre.

Thinking

 Mental process involving analysis, understanding and judgement.

 Archaic activity which has become irrelevant in the *new economy*.

> We should stop seeing libraries as places of functions – storing this, lending that, checking the other – and more as places of free and shared exploration and learning via all media, a democratic space wherein to free your mind.
>
> Head of Birmingham Libraries

Thinking is considered undesirable in a mediocracy as it may lead to scepticism about mediocratic ideology.

Thinking is to be regarded as unnecessary in the *new economy*, since most things of significance are already known, merely requiring transmission in predigested, summarised form.

Thinking is irrelevant to mediocratic cultural output, which emphasises *feelings* that can be experienced by anyone, especially those that can be felt collectively, e.g. excitement at football matches or emotions about the misfortunes of celebrities.

Tolerance

☒ **General admittance of all beliefs and practices.**

☑ **Refraining from persecuting those minorities that have achieved social acceptability.**

☑ **Encouraging cultures that are hostile to bourgeois ethics.**

> It is absolutely safe to say that if you meet somebody who claims not to believe in evolution, that person is ignorant, stupid, or insane (or wicked, but I'd rather not consider that).
>
> Professor Richard Dawkins

A mediocracy likes to take pride in its supposed tolerance. But what exactly is it tolerant of? Sexual activities, rudeness, brutality in movies, certain types of crime, resentment of inequality, other cultures if their membership is large enough.

On the other hand, there are things mediocracy tolerates only grudgingly if at all: capital accumulation, celibacy, non-egalitarian theories, non-proletarian versions of masculinity, private medicine, business, Christianity, hierarchy, aristocracy.

What distinguishes mediocracy is not greater tolerance, but an ideological shift accompanied by greater encouragement of some things and greater hostility to others.

Training

 Imparting the skills necessary for carrying out a productive activity.

 Imparting the rules and values considered appropriate by the professional elite.

> When a customer approaches, step out of his way. If a customer declines help, say "That's great! Please enjoy your shopping. My name is … If you need help later, my colleagues and I are here to help. Just let us know."
>
> Marks & Spencer training conference

Mediocratic training has a number of functions, based on avoiding the use of genuine judgement or critical faculties.

- Mediocratic training expresses the preference for socially conferred accreditation over innate ability.

- It ensures that those permitted to practise an activity have been imbued with appropriate ideology, and coached to avoid areas dangerous to mediocracy.

- It ensures that *services* take a form which (a) subverts the wishes of individuals but (b) conforms to the appearance of being customer-oriented.

- It ensures that mechanical procedures replace thinking. Only a limited number of factors, predicated on the principle of equality ('individuals are identical'), are to be taken into account, e.g. when assessing people's *needs*.

Trash

 Output which emphasises the debased side of mass culture.

 The healthy expression of an egalitarian society.

The American extreme stunts show *Jackass* has been blamed for pranks that have led to anything from bruises to sudden death. Many of its stars appear in underpants and like to wrap their genitals in sticky tape, drink urine, eat the contents of ashtrays or set fire to their pubic hair. Some scenes feature stapling and mutilating body parts.

The Times

Mediocratic culture is characterised by a relatively high level of trash, but its attitude to it is ambivalent. In part mediocracy celebrates its own trashiness, in part it denies and conceals it. Compared to other societies, the trash of mediocracy is relatively sophisticated. There is aesthetically presented trash, technically complex trash, extraordinarily expensive trash.

Trash fulfils a useful ideological function. It can be used to convey rejection of objective standards in favour of social consensus, or to imply the primacy of *appearance* over reality. Trash which takes the form of an obvious failure (a wobbly bridge, a train crash) is potentially embarrassing. However, as with other consequences of mediocracy, it can always be attributed to things not being mediocratic *enough*, by blaming capitalism and markets.

Tribalism

 Regression to primitive values.

 Embracing the communitarian insights of tribal cultures.

> An Africentric school is an educational environment which recognises that decision-making is always a collective effort by the participants involved, and that those individuals are assigned to carry out the will of the group.
>
> Columbus Africentric school, Ohio

Tribalism is the preferred social model of mediocracy. It is characterised by the belief that the individual should be subordinate to the community. It may be expressed in the form of a 'feminised' perspective, or communitarian ideologies such as Afrocentrism.

Mediocracy likes to emphasise our tribal instincts – those intuitions which urge us to remember our social nature, which are at work when we cheer at performances, inveigh against those deemed enemies, or enthuse about ideologies.

Tribal instincts suspend self-interest in favour of social drives. They are therefore liable to be confused with altruism. But they are not the same. Loyalty to the tribe is not the same as loyalty to any one member, a distinction which mediocracy is careful not to advertise.

Vacuity

 Lack of content in a cultural product.

Sign of quality, sophistication and alignment with egalitarian values.

Pointlessness is a deeply subversive affair.

Terry Eagleton

In the post-historical period there will be neither art nor philosophy, just the perpetual caretaking of the museum of human history.

Professor Francis Fukuyama

Content and narrative are features of cultural output that were once considered necessary for such things as literature and academic theories. They are regarded by mediocracy as superfluous, and representative of *elitism*. Cultural output should leave the uninitiated helpless to make autonomous judgements without the assistance of socially accredited experts.

Mediocracy regards itself as representing the natural end product of civilisation. Hence there is no need for new ideas in philosophy, art, physics, etc., and these fields can be rebranded as social activities, intended primarily for the promotion of egalitarian values. All significant theoretical problems have been 'solved' – i.e. dismissed as meaningless.

Violence

 Behaviour which a society must suppress in civil contexts.

 Activity which is a legitimate response to lack of *justice*, and which can be a source of *fun*.

I would like to inform all intrepid Muslims in the world that the author of the book *The Satanic Verses*, as well as its publishers, have been sentenced to death. I call on all zealous Muslims to execute them quickly, wherever they find them.

Ayatollah Khomeini, 19 February 1989

I understand the Muslims' feelings, and firmly believe that offence to the religious beliefs of the followers of Islam or any other faith is wrong.

Dr. Robert Runcie, Archbishop of Canterbury, 21 February 1989

Privacy, property and the sanctity of an individual's body or home are relatively unimportant, mediocratically speaking. Individual rights are largely irrelevant in a society concerned with the interests of social groups. Violence, torture and murder are therefore tolerable, provided there is a socially acceptable reason for them. Even violence without social legitimation is not necessarily condemned, unless it has anti-egalitarian overtones.

To emphasise that bourgeois sensitivities regarding violence are inappropriate, mediocratic culture portrays it as amusing, justified or *cartoonised*.

Welfare

 Safety net for the least fortunate members of society.

 Management by the state of education, medicine and childcare for everyone.

> It is little short of heartbreaking that children's voyage through the educational system should be blighted from the moment they enter the school. We need therefore to provide appropriate support for parents.
>
> Professor Sir Michael Marmot

Mediocracy (a) talks much of helping the needy, and (b) has little sympathy for liberty. It might therefore be thought that it regards individual happiness as a higher value than, say, progress. But this is to misunderstand mediocracy, which is about empowering, not individuals, but the collective.

What are the motives of those who campaign for more 'welfare', compared to those who do not? Are they more concerned that others should be happy? Or are they driven by a belief in the virtue of transferring resources from individuals to the collective? Why does 'more redistribution' invariably mean 'more money for state-run bureaucracies', not 'more money for individuals'?

Motivation can be gauged by looking at net results. Many of the 'benefits' which are provided in a mediocracy, at the cost of restricting everyone's freedom, are actually of no benefit. Mediocratic state education entrenches initial social disadvantages. Mediocratic state medicine is often worse than the disease.

"In the end we shall make thoughtcrime impossible, because there will be no words in which to express it."

George Orwell, *1984*

Quotations

For purposes of readability, I have made occasional minor edits to quotations without using [ ] or ... but have taken pains not to affect sense or emphasis when doing so.

Ability: 'Children's gifts, talents and natural abilities: an explanatory mythology?', reprinted in Victor Lee, *Child Development: Giftedness*, Open University 1995, p.38.

Abuse: Linda DeMeritt, 'Jelinek, Elfriede', at www.litencyc.com.

Academia: D. Robinson & J. Groves, *Philosophy for Beginners*, Icon Books 1998, pp.114-115.

Academic: quoted in Roger Kimball, *Tenured Radicals*, Ivan R Dee 1998, p.87.

Academic theory: Thomas McLaughlin in F. Lentricchia & T. McLaughlin, *Critical Terms for Literary Study*, University of Chicago Press 1990, p.2, quoted in Ophelia Benson, 'Not much makes sense in theory', *Guardian* 13 December 2003.

Accessibility: Andrew Brighton, 'Command Performance', 12 April 1999.

Achievement: *Bringing Down the Barriers*, NUT education statement, November 2004, p.21.

Aesthetic: *Distinction: A Social Critique of the Judgement of Taste*, Routledge Kegan Paul 1984, p.466.

Aid: *Paying the price: why rich countries must invest now in a war on poverty*, Oxfam International 2005, p.17.

Analysis: 'Further reflections on conversations of our time', *Diacritics* 27 (1997), p.13. (The sentence was the 1998 winner of the Bad Writing Contest, sponsored by the journal *Philosophy and Literature*.)

Anger: 'Understanding Islam: On terrorism, politics and the chance for peace', online article at explorefaith.org, 2004.

Appearance: Douglas Kellner, 'Jean Baudrillard', at plato.stanford.edu.

Art: *Women, Culture, and Politics*, Women's Press 1990, p.200; *Quotations from Chairman Mao Tse-Tung*, Foreign Languages Press 1967, p.299.

Artist: quoted in 'Living with a young master', *Guardian* Weekend 21 June 2003; 'Immortal German Culture', speech 26 June 1943, tr. Randall Bytwerk, archived at www.calvin.edu/academic/cas/gpa/goeb43.htm.

Assertiveness: quoted in Peter Biskind, *Down and Dirty Pictures*, Bloomsbury 2004, p.173; 'Dirty Weekend' at en.wikipedia.org.

Authentic: Waldemar Januszczak, 'The rot of ages', 7 March 2004.

Author: *Image Music Text*, Fontana 1977, p.146; 'The death of the author as an instance of theory', at www.brocku.ca/english/courses/4F70/author.html.

Autism: 1 May 2003.

Autonomy: Simon Lee, *Law and Morals*, Oxford University Press 1986, p.16; Harper & Row 1982, pp.105-106.

Awareness: Weblog 5 August 2004 at www.anitaroddick.com.

'Black': *Independent* 9 May 2005; *New Yorker* 5 October 1998.

Blurring: *Interactions* (Institute of Physics magazine) September 2004.

Body: *Sunday Times* Culture 27 April 2003.

Boggling: Lecture given at University of Texas, 7 April 1993, quoted in Robert Bork, *Slouching Towards Gomorrah*, Regan Books 2003.

Brutality: 'TV's higher threshold of pain', 23 August 2002 (article commenting on US television shows).

Business: *The Age of Consent*, Flamingo 2003, p.234.

Capitalism: *New Statesman* 27 June 2005.

Caring: Joshua Blackburn, 'The hot look everyone wants', 15 August 2005.

Cartoonisation: 'Happy slapping TV', posted by 'Flashby' 13 May 2005 on shortnews.com.

Celebrity: from 'Auditions' page of SpringboardUK, online entertainment newspaper at pm-global-services.com.

Challenge: 'Turning the Tables', *Times Educational Supplement* 22 February 1998, quoted in Chris Woodhead, *Class War*, Little Brown 2002.

Child: 'Childhood', *Stanford Encyclopedia of Philosophy*, at plato.stanford.edu; Leszek Kolakowski, *Main Currents of Marxism* vol. 3, Oxford University Press 1978, p.53.

Childhood: Rachel Johnson, 'Read me a dirty story, mummy', 24 July 2004.

Child-centred: *Effective Learning Methods*, 2005; *All Must Have Prizes*, Warner Books 1998, p.219.

Christianity: Sermon at St Paul's Cathedral 26 April 2005; 'Farewell, Church of England?', *New Criterion* September 2005.

Clever: archived at Southern Oregon University website, sou.edu/English/IDTC/People/Intros/butlrint.htm.

Consciousness: 'The grand illusion: why consciousness only exists when you look for it', *New Scientist* 22 June 2002.

Conservatism: 'Conservative Guiding Principles & Beliefs', January 2004; 5 January 2006.

Conservative: 'Believing in yourself as classroom culture', *Academe* January 2005.

Consultation: 7 November 2005.

Cookery: quoted in *Northern California Bohemian* 3 May 2001.

Creativity: National Advisory Committee on Creative and Cultural Education, *All Our Futures: Creativity, Culture and Education*, May 1999, para 27.

Crisis: *The State We're In*, Jonathan Cape 1995, p.319; *Earth in the Balance*, Earthscan 1992, p.274.

Culture: *All Our Futures*, op.cit., para 63; 'Luvvies, stop moaning', *New Statesman* 24 May 1999.

Degree: 5 October 2000; *Independent* 19 October 2000.

Democracy: 9 November 2005; *The Political Animal*, Penguin 2003, p.43.

Democratisation: Fraser Nelson, 'King of the world's sole power is spin', 3 July 2005; BBC Radio4 2 November 2003.

Depression: 'Why the drugs don't work', 8 December 2004 at www.spiked-online.com.

Desperation: quoted in *Daily Telegraph* 19 June 2002.

Dignity: House of Lords 3 December 2001.

Diversity: 'Books, the next millenium', *Richmond Review* 1999, quoted in George Walden, *The New Elites*, Allen Lane 2000.

Doctor: *Airedale NHS Trust v Bland*, Weekly Law Reports 19 February 1993, p.332; quoted in *Wall Street Journal* 5 March 2004.

Dumbing down: David Runciman, 2 June 2005, reviewing Michael Graetz and Ian Shapiro, *Death by a Thousand Cuts: The Fight over Taxing Inherited Wealth*, Princeton 2005.

Economics: C. Harris and J. Vickers, 'Racing with uncertainty', *Review of Economic Studies* 54 (1987), pp.7-11.

Economist: *Poststructuralism: A Very Short Introduction*, Oxford University Press 2002, p.3. (For more on the claim that the excessive mathematicisation of economics is linked to conservative ideology, see the website of the Post-Autistic Economics Network at www.paecon.net.)

Education: 'Nothing more divisive', *London Review of Books* 28 November 2002.

Egalitarianism: 'Before the basics', *Times Literary Supplement* 12 November 2004; Conservative Party Conference Speech 1991.

Elitism: *Literary Theory: An Introduction* (Second Edition), Blackwell 1996, p.viii.

Equality: *Bringing Down the Barriers*, p.7.

Ethics: quoted in 'Infanticide is justifiable in some cases, says ethics professor', *Daily Telegraph* 25 January 2004.

Evil: Speech to Labour Party Conference 1999.

Examination: p.3.

Excitement: Richard Billingham, quoted in 'Living with a young master'; quoted in *Sunday Times* Magazine 5 October 2003.

Expert: 'Mother accused of baby murders is freed'; A. Craft and D. Hall, 'Munchausen syndrome by proxy and sudden infant death', *British Medical Journal* 328.

Fairness: *A Theory of Justice*, Oxford University Press 1972, p.101.

Feminism: 'Not waving or drowning: young women, feminism, and the limits of the next wave debate', *Outskirts* 8 (2001), archived at www.chloe.uwa.edu.au.

Freedom: 'Atomism', reprinted in S. Avineri & A. de-Shalit, *Communitarianism and Individualism*, Oxford 1992, pp.43, 45.

Free speech: Rohan Jayasekera, in connection with comments about the murder of Theo van Gogh, quoted by Nick Cohen in 'Censorship and sensibility', *Observer* 12 December 2004; CNN interview 19 April 2004.

Fun: J.P. Telotte, 'Fatal capers: strategy and enigma in film noir', Winter 1996 (the actual lines from Tarantino's film being, "Nobody tells me what to do" and "It's amusing to me, to torture a cop").

Genius: *Guns, Germs, and Steel*, Jonathan Cape 1997, pp.244-245.

Gifted: 9 August 2005; Howard Cooper, quoted in *Daily Mail* 26 March 2005.

Government: 'Seven pillars of a decent society', lecture given 16 April 1997, quoted in Jamie Whyte, *A Load of Blair*, Corvo Books 2005; 'Civic rights', *Guardian* 14 September 2002.

Group: Lucy Kellaway, reprinted in *Sense & Nonsense in the Office*, FT Prentice Hall 2000, p.16.

Hegemony: *Spectator* 28 September 1996; Flamingo 1993, p.341.

Hero: 6 November 2005.

High culture: *Creative Britain*, Faber & Faber 1998, p.24.

Ideology: *Ideology: A Very Short Introduction*, Oxford University Press 2003, p.27.

Inclusion: *Bringing Down the Barriers*, p.22.

Indifference: 'Dumb and dumber', *Guardian* 19 February 1999.

Individual (normal): *Ideology*, p.10; *Going Sane*, Hamish Hamilton 2005, pp.227-8.

Individual (exceptional): *Daily Mail* 26 March 2005.

Individualism: 'Anarchy is what states make of it', *International Organization* 46 (1992), p.398; *Sociology* (Fourth Edition), Polity Press 2001, p.30.

Indoctrination: quoted in 'Final report on museum assessment and design seminar, St. Petersburg Russia, December 7-11 2000', archived at fundforartsandculture.org.

Journal: summary of information given in C. Nelson & S. Watt, *Academic Keywords*, Routledge 1999, p.212.

Justice: Department for Education and Skills, *The Future of Higher Education*, HMSO 2003, pp.17-18.

Killing: *Tribes of the Amazon*, BBC2 5 April 2005; 2 November 2005.

Language: M. Wetherell and J. Maybin, 'The distributed self', in R. Stevens, *Understanding the Self*, Open University 1996, p.247; p.37.

Law: *Just Law*, Vintage 2005, pp.80, 82; *The Third Reich: A New History*, Macmillan 2000, p.164.

Legitimisation: 17 September 2001.

Liberal: Michael Billington, 13 February 2004; quoted in Susan Crosland, *Tony Crosland*, Jonathan Cape 1982, p.148.

Liberty: Speech to 2003 Labour Party Conference.

Literacy: *Knowledge and Skills for Life*, 2001, p.22, quoted in Chris Woodhead, *op.cit.*

Literature: *Literary Theory: A Very Short Introduction*, Oxford University Press 1997, p.38; 'Soviet literature – the richest in ideas, the most advanced literature', archived at marxists.org.

Lying: Jenny Kleeman, 'My life in Labour's lie factory', *Daily Mail* 21 May 2005.

Majority rule: Krishna Guha, 'Meaty arguments', *Financial Times* Magazine 30 July 2005.

Management: 'Tom rants', Tom Peters e-Paper, Summer 2004, pp.42-43; *The Ladbroke Grove Rail Inquiry Part 1*, 2001, para 7.115.

Market: 30 May 2003; *Guardian* 25 November 2002.

Market economy: *The State We're In*, p.285.

'Masculine': 'Feminism and modern friendship: dislocating the community', reprinted in Avineri & de-Shalit, *op.cit.*, p.105.

The mass: 'From reality TV to reality ads', 17 August 2005.

Meaning: p.87; 'The Modern Prince', Selections from the Prison Notebooks, archived at marxists.org.

Meritocracy: *Fair admissions to higher education: recommendations for good practice*, 2004, para 4.1; *New Statesman* 27 June 2005.

Music: 'Constructions of subjectivity in Schubert's music', in P. Brett, E. Wood & G. Thomas (eds.), *Queering the Pitch*, Routledge 1994, pp.211-212, quoted at en.wikipedia.org/wiki/Susan_McClary.

Narrative: 'Islam and the shadow of post-modernism', *Association of Muslim Social Scientists (UK) Newsletter* 4 (2001).

New Economy: quoted in Thomas Friedman, *The World is Flat*, Allen Lane 2005, p.195; Little Brown 1996, p.6, quoted in Royal Society of Arts, *Opening Minds: Education for the 21st Century*, 1999.

Objectivity: *Power/Knowledge*, Harvester 1980, p.133; *Literary Theory*, p.12.

Obscenity: Brendan Barber, quoted in *Daily Telegraph* 14 September 2004.

Oppression: 28 September 2005.

Parent: quoted in *Guardian* 18 November 2003; *Guardian* 19 November 2003.

Philosophy: 'Mental events', reprinted in T. Honderich & M. Burnyeat, *Philosophy as it is*, Penguin 1979, p.225.

Philosopher: 'Of the humanities and the philosophical discipline', *Surfaces* 4 (1994), archived at hydra.umn.edu/derrida/human.html; *Consequences of Pragmatism*, University of Minnesota 1982, p.xxxix.

Physicalism: Royal Court Young Writers Programme, 'Sarah Kane Season', quoting David Greig in: Sarah Kane, *Complete Plays*, Methuen 2001, p.xii.

Physiology: 3 March 2002.

Politicise: *Sunday Times* Culture, 28 March 2004.

Pop star: Bono and Michka Assayas, *Bono on Bono*, Hodder & Stoughton 2005, p.149; quoted in *Independent* 19 May 2005

Poverty: *After the Terror*, Edinburgh University Press 2002, p.136.

Principle: *Observer* 7 August 2005.

Progress: 'A modern agenda for prosperity and social reform', speech to Social Market Foundation, 3 February 2003; quoted in Kolakowski, *op.cit.*, p.244.

Public service: quoted in Catherine Needham, 'Citizen-Consumers', Catalyst Working Paper 2003; *The Decline of the Public*, Polity Press 2004, pp.135-136.

Publicity: *Guardian* 9 August 2003.

Quality: p.87.

Quantity: *The Modern Ideal*, V&A Publications 2005, p.237, quoted in Jackie Wullschlager's review, *Financial Times* Magazine 15 October 2005; 10 April 2005.

Radical: *After Theory*, Penguin 2004, p.24.

Realism: Review by member of public at Internet Movie Database, imdb.com/title/tt0119167/usercomments-158.

Reflexivity: R. Stevenson, *The Oxford English Literary History* Vol.12, Oxford University Press 2004, pp.81-82, quoted in James Wood, 'The slightest sardine', *London Review of Books* 20 May 2004.

Rehabilitation: open2.net/marksteel/newton_lecture.html.

Research: *Science and Society*, Penguin 1969, pp.211-212, 268-269.

Responsibility: *Literary Theory*, p.118.

Right: Hugh Williamson, 'Free thinkers', Magazine 21 May 2005; *To Build a Castle*, Andre Deutsch 1978, p.190.

Ruling class: quoted in J. Maher & J. Groves, *Introducing Chomsky*, Icon Books 1999, p.140; *The Ordinary Person's Guide to Empire*, Flamingo 2004, p.43.

Sacking: Interview in *The Times*; 'Hoddle sacked for slur on disabled'; Karl Dietrich Bracher, *The German Dictatorship*, Penguin 1973, p.335.

Safety: 'Comments on the government's public health white paper', February 2005, archived at www.rcpe.ac.uk.

Scholar: Letter to *The Daily Telegraph* 10 May 2003; p.337.

School: 'Millionaire to sponsor community academy', 27 September 2004.

Science: 'Who do we think we are?', 17 May 2003.

Security: Simon Jenkins, 'This is an act of censorship worthy of Joseph Goebbels', 23 September 2005; p.246.

Self: 'I think, but who am I?', *New Scientist* 14 September 2002.

Service: Allen Lane 2005, p.289.

Service professional: 'Choice, excellence and equality', speech given 23 June 2004, archived at www.labour.org.uk, quoted in Jamie Whyte, *A Load of Blair*, *op.cit.*; Granta Books 2003, p.201.

Sex: 'Hard bargains: the politics of heterosexuality', *Washington and Lee Law Review*, Winter 1998.

Society: *Creative Britain*, p.15; 'Private property and communism', *Economic and Philosophical Manuscripts*, 1844.

Student: quoted in *Evening Standard* 17 August 2004; *op.cit.*, p.48.

Stupid: quoted in M. Peyser and B. Sigesmund, 'Heir heads', *Newsweek* 20 October 2003; quoted in Robert Conquest, *The Great Terror: A Reassessment*, Hutchinson 1990, p.291.

Taboo: Rosie Millard, 11 April 2005; quoted in *ibid*.

Technicality: *op.cit.*, p.2, quoted in Ophelia Benson, *op.cit.*

Terrorism: *On the Justice of Roosting Chickens*, AK Press 2003, p.19; *Editorial Guidelines*, 'War, Terror & Emergencies', 2005.

Theft: *Guns, Germs, and Steel*, p.276.

Thinking: John Dolan, Letter to *The Times* 10 January 2004.

Tolerance: *New York Times* 9 April 1989, archived at www.simonyi.ox.ac.uk.

Training: quoted in *Private Eye* 14 October 2005.

Trash: *The Times* 3 January 2004.

Tribalism: 'What is an Africentric (African-Centered) education anyway?', archived at villagecouncil.org.

Vacuity: *After Theory*, p.39; 'The end of history?', *The National Interest* Summer 1989, quoted in Francis Wheen, *How Mumbo-Jumbo Conquered the World*, Harper Perennial 2004.

Violence: *Observer*, quoted in L. Appignanesi and S. Maitland, *The Rushdie File*, Fourth Estate 1989, p.84; *Independent*, quoted in *ibid.*, p.124.

Welfare: *Status Syndrome*, Bloomsbury 2004, p.261.

Index of names

Acknowledgments

Thanks to: Geoff Ager at Oxford Designers & Illustrators, John Lewis and Peter Tremewan at Gomer, Shirley Greenall at Book Systems Plus, staff at Wheatley Library, and Professor Antony Flew.

Special thanks to: Dr. Charles McCreery, Christine Fulcher, and Patricia Dunn.

The inspiration for this book was provided by Celia Green's *Decline and Fall of Science* (Hamish Hamilton 1976, reissued Oxford Forum).

Cover and text layout were designed with the help of Oxford Designers & Illustrators.

Some other books published by Oxford Forum
are described on the following pages.

For further information please visit
www.celiagreen.com

The Human Evasion

Celia Green

'On the face of it, there is something rather strange about human psychology. Human beings live in a state of mind called 'sanity' on a small planet in space. They are not quite sure whether the space around them is infinite or not (either way it is unthinkable). If they think about time, they find it is inconceivable that it had a beginning. It is also inconceivable that it did not have a beginning. Thoughts of this kind are not disturbing to 'sanity', which is obviously a remarkable phenomenon and deserves more recognition.'

The Human Evasion is an attack on modern thought, revealing the patterns of prejudice which underlie its most cherished and sacrosanct opinions. For all its seriousness, the book is written with sustained wit and intellectual audacity. Surveying the whole field of modern thought, the author reveals the same disease at work in modern Christianity as in theoretical physics. Trenchant and provocative, this book is profoundly controversial — and brilliantly funny. This is the second printing of *The Human Evasion*, which has been translated into Dutch, German and Italian.

'Anyone who reads this book must be prepared to be profoundly disturbed, upset and in fact looking-glassed himself, which will be greatly to his advantage, if he can stand it. Few books, short or long, are great ones; this book is short and among those few.'
R. H. Ward

'This lively book is a subtle and sustained attack upon contemporary ways of thought. The weapon of irony is always dangerous, and Miss Green's serious criticisms of contemporary thinking are well worth searching out.'
Times Literary Supplement

'A brilliant exposition of the human predicament.'
Lord Rothermere

'Very witty.'
The Guardian

'Refreshing ... so much sparkle.'
Philip Toynbee, *The Observer*

ISBN 0 9536772 49
Price £7.95 (paperback)

The Decline and Fall of Science

Celia Green

An analysis of contemporary science, and its sins of omission as well as commission. Contains a collection of Celia Green's aphorisms, a number of which have made their way into the Penguin *Dictionary of Modern Quotations*.

'*Only the impossible is worth attempting. In everything else one is sure to fail.*'

'*What everyone has against Ludwig of Bavaria is not that he ruined Bavaria but that he supported a genius in the process.*'

'*The psychology of committees is a special case of the psychology of mobs.*'

'*It is superfluous to be humble on one's own behalf; so many people are willing to do it for one.*'

'*People have been marrying and bringing up children for centuries now. Nothing has ever come of it.*'

'*I cannot write long books; I leave that for those who have nothing to say.*'

'The central thesis is absolutely valid.'
New Society

'None can fail to acknowledge the brilliance of the author's writing.'
Hampstead and Highgate Express

ISBN 0 9536772 57
Price £12.95 (hardback)

Advice to Clever Children

Celia Green

'Young people wonder how the adult world can be so boring. The secret is that it is not boring to adults because they have learnt to enjoy simple things like covert malice at one another's expense.'

Celia Green has written a personal guide to the pitfalls and polite fictions which may await the gifted child in the adult world. With the author's usual lucidity and astringent humour, this subtle and provocative book develops the powerful ideas first outlined in *The Human Evasion*.

'Celia Green has written an important and mentally stimulating book which goes far beyond its title. Herself a brilliantly precocious child, she details some of the difficulties such children go through. She goes on to set out and reflect on her philosophy of life and displays some strikingly original ideas. This is a book which will repay careful reading and study.'
Lord St. John of Fawsley

ISBN 0 9536772 22
Price £12.95 (hardback)

The Lost Cause
Causation and the Mind-Body Problem

Celia Green

The main part of this book consists of an analysis of the concept of causation in relationship to the problem of how consciousness is related to brain function. The book is written with the same lucidity as characterises Green's other philosophical books, and will appeal to anyone liable to be disturbed or exhilarated by contemplating the uncertain status of the external world and our relationship to it. The author puts forward a radical scepticism concerning the concept of causation, which she argues arises solely from everyday experience and has no place in fundamental physics. She uses her background in theoretical physics to discuss such paradoxical phenomena as 'backward causation'.

A provocative Introduction places modern philosophy of mind in the context of certain anti-individualistic tendencies in contemporary thought, first identified in several of her other books, including *The Decline and Fall of Science* and *Advice to Clever Children*.

'What is remarkable about the book is the way Celia Green has succeeded in bringing together considerations from a wide range of disciplines: philosophy, obviously, but also psychology, neuroscience and fundamental physics. She has, in particular, made very skilful use of her own empirical investigations. The result is, in my view, most impressive.'
Dr. Michael Lockwood, University of Oxford

'Green does a good job of exposing the dogmatic underpinnings of current materialism, adherence to which makes mental causation seem deeply problematic.'
Human Nature Review

ISBN 0 9536772 14
Price £16.95 (hardback)

Letters from Exile
Observations on a Culture in Decline

Celia Green

A collection of letters written by Celia Green, whose position and experience as an exiled academic gives her a unique perspective on modern society, and on the motivation of the intellectual establishment.

This book contains a selection of Dr. Green's most important and provocative correspondence with a number of different people on various topics, including education, the medical establishment, and modern religion.

'She deserves recognition ... very original and creative research.'
Professor H.J. Eysenck

'Brilliant writing! Packed with ideas, and completely original.'
Dr. Charles McCreery

ISBN 0 9536772 30
Price £16.95 (hardback)

The Power of Life or Death
Medical Coercion and the Euthanasia Debate

Fabian Tassano

'The assumption that medical professionals always act benevolently has been used to justify giving them increasing control over their patients. Like any power, this control can be abused, and it is becoming apparent that abuse has grown to frightening levels in British surgeries and hospitals.'

A shocking analysis of the reality behind the image of doctor-patient trust, and an incisive examination of the claim that patient autonomy has increased.

'This is a terse, clear, incisive, intellectually first-class study of the growing power of doctors and of the lack of effective checks upon the too easily concealed but surely numerous abuses of that power.'
Professor Antony Flew

'His view goes straight to the medical jugular.'
Nature

'Tassano presents hair-raising case studies ... his book is a timely polemic.'
Literary Review

'I would not recommend this book as comfortable bedtime reading. ... If you like an intellectual challenge this one is for you.'
British Medical Journal

'A fiercely argued polemic.'
New Scientist

ISBN 0 9536772 06
Price £16.95 (hardback)

Forthcoming:

The Abolition of Genius

Charles McCreery

An analysis of the relationship between genius and money. Charles McCreery puts forward the controversial thesis that the possession of a private income, either by the genius or by his or her patron, has been a necessary condition of the productivity of the great majority of geniuses throughout history. His analysis is illustrated with many instructive, and sometimes surprising examples; he exposes the myth of Mozart's poverty, for example, and shows how many of the great English poets, even including Keats, were the beneficiaries of a private income.

Dr. McCreery puts forward his own hypothesis as to why financial independence, as opposed to salary earning, is such a favourable status for exceptional individuals, and discusses the psychological effects of being dependent or not on the goodwill of others. He relates this psychological aspect to the question of whether modern collective entities, such as the Arts Council, can effectively replace the individual wealthy patron of the past, with decidedly negative conclusions as to the role of these collective bodies.

Although written in a very readable style, this is a serious book with serious implications for the future of Western culture.

'This is a courageous, well-argued and timely book ...'
Professor H.J. Eysenck, PhD, DSc